UNDER GROWTH

The UEA Undergraduate Creative
Writing Anthology 2015

UNDERGROWTH

First published by Egg Box Publishing 2015

International ©2015 retained
by individual authors.

A CIP record for this book is available
from the British Library.

Undergrowth is typeset in Adobe
Garamond. Titles are set in Bebas.

Printed and bound in the
UK by Imprint Digital.

Designed and typeset by Sean Purdy.

Proofread by Imogen Lees.

Distributed by Central Books.

ISBN: 978-0-9932962-0-8

EDITORS' NOTE

IN THIS, THE UNDERGRADUATE ANTHOLOGY'S SECOND YEAR, we decided to expand its scope by opening submissions to all students in the School of Literature, Drama and Creative Writing, as well as to creative writers in the School of Art, Media and American Studies. Why did we do this? Well, for one thing, we did it in the interests of collegiality, and to nod to the fact that writing relationships and alliances form and exist across disciplinary boundaries. For another, we wanted to include as many writers in the process as possible, in order to represent work of the highest quality. Between these covers you will therefore find some of the very best poetry and prose produced by UEA undergraduates.

There is little more to be said by way of introduction other than a huge thank you to:

Philip Langeskov, Nathan Hamilton at Egg Box Publishing and Sean Purdy.

We would also like to thank the following students who assisted with the selection and editing of work:

Caitlin Arthur, Danielle Ball, Freddie Bettles-Lake, Isis Billing, Sara Helen Binney, Peter Bloxham, Megan Bradbury, Claire Browne, Grace Carman, Cathy Davies, Amy Fancourt, Joanna Hollins, Jonathan Horvath, Paul Howarth, Joe Innes, Sarah A. Jones, Sean Wai Keung, Zoe Kingsley, Miranda Langford, Eve Lacroix, Sophie Marner, Erin Michie, Emma Miller, Faye Milton, Catherine Momoh, Molly Morris, Imogen Orchard, Simon Pook, Claire Reiderman, Alice Rodgers,

Rachel Sammons, Bikram Sharma, Silvia Sheehan, Susannah Smith, Stoyo Stoev, Sara Taylor, Jo Thompson and Nathaniel Woo.

We hope you enjoy your time in the Undergrowth.

The Editorial Team
Adam White, Ana Dukakis, Cleo Stead, Emma Mackilligin, Francesca Kritikos, Leo Temple

May 2015

CONTENTS

IN MEMORY OF REBECCA MCMANUS

R EBECCA MCMANUS WAS A FINAL YEAR ENGLISH LITERATURE WITH Creative Writing student when she died in May 2014

'It was my great pleasure to supervise Rebecca's (1st Class) poetry dissertation. Very few of her poems needed much in the way of editing; she wrote often and she wrote well. In my feedback on her writing I noted that in her poems 'The theme of the sky is so open as to be a way of looking, not just up but out from a self...drawing our attention to things on the periphery of the horizon, whether vapour trails or loss.' Rebecca's poems are quietly intense; an individual observation but universally recognisable in the burnished details; piano notes, jewelled saints, a blank sky. A real poet, visceral, quietly insistent, sharply intelligent, with language and detail both rich and enriching, her writing is borne out of a humane imagination where seeing is a kind of faith and words are epiphany.'
 – Andrea Holland

'Gentle, clever, funny, inventive and kind, Rebecca McManus was a truly special young woman, whose loss is felt by everyone who had the privilege of knowing her. Her red beret and gorgeous, funky clothes were like little flags of the spirit and brightness and character and quiet sense of humour within. This Anthology is dedicated to her memory.'
 – Clare Connors

HEAVEN ON EARTH

On days when the washing machine
drowns out your thoughts

When people play piano
to the muted beat of raindrops

When jewelled saints
appear in your dreams

When the sky is absent
and life must be present:

Where is heaven if not here?

UNDER GROWTH

WEEDKILLER

I thought you were a weed.
Fallopia japonica, a spreading
pest. A vine creeping into
stories that weren't about you.

The more I smother you,
the more you spring back –
a contrary dandelion
growing up through cracks.

No matter how much herbicide I
apply, your roots won't shrink,
won't wither away. You overturn
other men like broken slabs.

You're no weed, even thistles
aren't this stubborn. White like
convolvulus – a throttling ghost. I
should exorcise myself of you.

LUCAS ALDRICH

SCULPTING WITH COLOUR

'**S**ORRY I'M LATE. I'VE GOT A FLIGHT IN TWO HOURS.'
'*C'est bon*, it's okay.'
'Unfortunately we're going to have to keep this quite short. Do you mind if I put this on the table? It's to record the conversation.'
'Sure, no problem. I'm sorry for all the mess.'
'Don't worry about it. How long have you lived here?'
'*En Paris?* Ever since I left *La Maison Du Rêve*, fifty years ago. That was where he lived, in those final years. The House of Dreams. Isn't that beautiful?'
'Was it nice to live there?'
'Oh yes. Yes it was wonderful. I felt like a princess. I had a pretty little room, overlooking the garden. He kept the paintings of his, ahh, *comment tu dit?* His "colleagues", yes. He kept all their paintings in my room. One week I would put up a Picasso, the next I would swap it for one of Duchamp's. It was like having my own little gallery.'
'So he treated you well?'
'*Bien sûr,* of course. He was like a father to me.'
'Many people have wondered at how... well, I've seen pictures of you when you were younger. You were very beautiful–'
'"Were?" *Merci.*'
'Oh, no, no. I only meant–'
'It's okay. Relax, *monsieur*. I was only, ahh, "pulling your leg."'
'Oh, right. Sorry. It's just, sitting here surrounded by all these amazing artifacts you have in your apartment, I'm a little star struck. I mean, is that you in the portrait?'
'Yes. You recognize it, *non?*'

'It can't be a Dali, can it?'

'Ah close, *mais non*. It is the other great surrealist, Man Ray. I was curating a gallery of *Maître's* work in Paris when I met him. He had such dark eyes; I was a little scared when first I saw him, I must admit. I didn't know who he was at first; I thought he wanted something terrible with me! He was one of the sweetest men I ever knew, though. Although the first time he painted me, he painted my body as if it was a mountain. As you can imagine, I was not pleased.'

'And that? That's a cutout, isn't it?'

'Ah yes, this is my most prized possession. He gave it to me a week before I left. I could tell he was sad when he gave it to me, which was very unusual. I had never seen him unhappy in his workshop, surrounded by his art. But this morning, he looked so sad in his wheelchair, holding this little paper heart in his hands. I think he knew then that I would be leaving. Lydia had probably said something to him. Of course, I didn't realize until later that she was the one who said I had to go.'

'That must have made you pretty angry.'

'At the time, yes, but this was only because I did not know why I had to leave. When I understood what must have happened, I did not resent her for it. She was with him before me, and she was with him after me, and after all the others, until the end. It was a beautiful year; I would have felt privileged to have experienced just one month.'

'Tell me about it then, that year with him.'

'Okay. Where should I start?'

'Well, the article is for his hundredth birthday, so shall we start with the first time you met?'

*

'It was 1948, summer. I was the caretaker of a dressmaker's young daughter and we had gone for a walk. We found ourselves by a beautiful garden. The flowers, they seemed to bind and expand together. They created this... this incredible, blinding explosion of pure colour. In the centre of all this he sat, perfectly still except for the brush in his hand. I think this must have been one of the last times he painted; I never saw him at an easel in our time together. *J'ai été captivé*. I could not take my eyes off him. The way he was using the brush, slashing away at the canvas as if without thought, it was like he was... was possessed.

I wanted to call out to him, but he was so entranced by his work that I did not want to disturb him. Instead I wrote him a letter asking if I could meet him. The next day I received his reply saying, "Come and see me."

When I first met him, he exclaimed immediately, *"Mon Dieu!* This dress, it is exquisite. The colour, it embraces my eyes like an old friend." This was a very Matisse expression, you know? He had such a wonderful way of describing the world, its shades and hues in particular. He could give life to the most listless grey; brighten the darkest black, just by his words.

I know I talk of it often but you must understand, for Matisse, colour was life. This has remained with me, this belief. You can see it in my art also. There are very few paintings of mine that have dull shades in them… the *joy* of the others.

Je m'égare, I am getting distracted. Yes, he was very complimentary of my dress, and I was very flattered. He told me that he had asked me to come see him, as he would be returning to his villa in Venice soon. He wondered if I would like to come work for him as an assistant. I think I must have looked like I was going to fall over as his expression became worried. I jumped and shouted, "Yes, yes, yes!"

"Bon," he said, "I will expect you there on Monday."

"Thank you *monsieur,* thank you!" I began to leave when he called, "One moment, Jaqueline. You must talk to Lydia first."

"Pourquoi, monsieur?"

"Just to talk. She is in the next room."

"Okay."

She was in the room next to his studio, and was waiting for me when I entered. I have never seen a woman who was so effortlessly glamorous. Her blonde hair shimmered in the light as beautifully as the diamonds that hung from her ears, and her black dress looked like something a *debutante* might wear. I was quite intimidated, you can imagine *non?*

"Bonjour, madame." She looked at me for a long time. I felt as if she was, ahh, studying my body, memorizing every aspect of it.

Eventually she said, *"Bon,* you will do. I am the governess. I will have a room ready for you when you arrive on Sunday. Do not be late."

"But, *Monsieur* Matisse said…"

"I know what he said, he does not realize that you will need a day to get settled before he starts driving you like a mule."

Not knowing what else to say, I simply replied *"Merci, madame."* and began to leave.

She called after me as I left, "And you must call him *Maître* in the workshop." Master, this means. "This is not something he requests, I demand it. *Tu compris?"*

"Oui, madame." I left the studio, still excited but now a little… nervous also.

Lydia greeted me at the door when I arrived at *La Maison Du Rêve* and showed me to my room.

"You may make yourself dinner from anything in the kitchen. I'm sure you will want to sleep soon."

"Sleep? But it is only seven."

"You begin at six o'clock tomorrow morning. If you are late, you will not last long here."

I was surprised, but had already learned to do what Lydia said. I'm sure that's why I lasted so long there. The other assistants over the years were asked to leave within months; you know this, yes?

The next morning, I entered his workshop. Never have I seen so much colour in a place. The floor, it was like a mad party. Reds danced with greens, oranges embraced blues. It was madness. The walls were filled with colour also, but much more controlled. Covering one entire wall were the shapes of plants and fruit, life bursting from the greens and blues and oranges and yellows that coloured them. I did not know it at the time but this was the beginning of *The Parakeet and The Mermaid*; it was only missing the title characters.

Matisse was looking at these shapes intently. As I approached he did not notice me, so intent was he on the wall. I stood quietly close by, waiting for him to recognize my presence. Finally he looked at me.

"Let's get started."

You mentioned earlier that people often suspected Matisse of... impure motives in hiring the others and myself. As you said I was young, beautiful by all accounts. The other assistants were too, of course. However, this had nothing to do with sexuality. To keep up with Matisse, you had to be young and fit. He was relentless. Never have I seen so much energy pour out of someone, especially not a man confined to a wheelchair. He used a pair of very large scissors. Just like when I saw him painting in the garden, he did not appear to think about the way he was cutting at all. He simply snipped and slashed at a furious pace. Colours fell to the floor like some magical blizzard as he chipped away at the paper. Once he had the shape he would hand it to me and I would race up the ladder that leant against the wall and pin it in the precise position and orientation that he desired. By the time I had placed it and reached the bottom of the stairs, he would have another shape ready. It was very tiring work, but I would get so caught up in his... his ecstasy, that I would hardly notice my own body's exhaustion.

This was what almost every day was like at the House of Dreams. Wake up as early as the sunrise, work without break for hours, before retiring well in to the evening. He treated me much like a daughter.

Sometimes we would have some champagne together in the evening, but he would always give me a half a glass and laugh, "You're too young to learn to drink!"

As I said earlier, there were very few times I can recall when he was not positively euphoric creating his art. Over the next year, he would put on wild jazz music while we worked and in the few breaks we took, I would be so overcome by the combination of exhaustion and excitement that I would be compelled to dance and jump and laugh. He would watch me and laugh as well. In his workshop, he was the happiest man alive.

I think this is what made Lydia so jealous. She felt excluded. Of course, she wanted Matisse to be happy, but she was never able to spend any time with us in the *atelier*, except for a few brief moments a day, so concerned was she with his business affairs. While he was in the workshop, he had not a care in the world and it must have hurt her to not be able to participate in his joy.

At this point, he suffered terrible insomnia after finding out. The result was that, in the night, he became a scared and malignant man. I would often hear him shouting abuse at Lydia while I was in bed. I'm sure I heard weeping too, but from who I do not know. This is why I do not resent her for what she did. Can you imagine? She had been with him for almost twenty years when I came. Their relationship was not sexual, I'm sure of that; it was much deeper I think. But to watch the man you love be so happy with another, younger, woman... especially when he was so vile to her most of the time? I cannot begin to think of the pain it must have caused her, but I know she kept a packed suitcase in her room, for when she could handle it no more.

Despite this, I was confused when *Maître* told me I could no longer stay at the villa. I did not quite understand what he was saying at first.

"*Pourquoi, Maître?* Do you need my room for something? I could sleep on the sofa if needed."

"I am sorry, *mon chéri.* I mean you cannot be here at all anymore."

I could not say anything. It was as if someone had punched me in the stomach, *tu compris?*

"I'm sorry, I cannot explain it. But you must leave. We have rented you an apartment in Nice where you can stay as long as you need. Goodbye."

With that he turned away from me and became intent on his colours. I stood still for a few moments, hoping he would turn back around laughing, a silly prank. But he did not. I packed my suitcase and left. I did not see Lydia anywhere. It was a very sad moment for me, but it was one of the most incredible years of my life and I will love that man forever.'

'So you're not angry with him for choosing Lydia over you?'

'Hah! Don't be ridiculous, *monsieur*. He enjoyed my company, I think I feel justified in saying he even liked me. But in his eyes, I was nothing compared to Lydia.'

'So they stayed together?'

'Oh yes. She sat next to his bed as he took his last breath. And when he was gone, she took that packed suitcase, and never returned to Venice.'

'You never saw him again?'

'*Non*. He died just four years later. But I take this little heart with me wherever I go. My little cutout.'

DARA ARAD

JUNGLE CLUB

YOU WATCH MOWGLI ON THE OTHER SIDE OF THE ROOM as he struggles to light the incense stick he's pinned into some crack in the ceiling panel. You know Isaac's watching too, that's part of the reason you watch. Most things after sunset are a struggle for Mowgli – when it gets dark he gets fucked, a well-kept routine. It's been like this since you found him on the grass outside your house four months ago, around the time things got hard with Isaac. You were walking home from another cyclical conversation and finding a boy you didn't know sitting there so helpless and harmless was just what you needed to pull you out of the cycle: a centrifugal force. His shirt was unbuttoned and he smelt of rum and smoke. He didn't get up so you joined him on the grass and instead of asking who he was or how he got there you just started to tell him everything Isaac was doing wrong or wasn't doing right. Hearing it aloud was weird. When you finished speaking he lit a cigarette and asked, "Who the fuck is Isaac?" He told you his name was Sam and gave you his digits – "Hit me up some time, my house throws dope parties."

Once lit, the incense releases a strong woody smell that doesn't seem congruous with the room's artificial light or 120bpm-electro-chillwave-soundtrack. It's too organic. You crinkle your nose and turn to Isaac. He raises an eyebrow to signal his agreement. Still watching Mowgli, who has now pulled the incense out of the crack and is waving it in this girl's face, Isaac gets right into your ear and whispers, "Case in point," and you know what he means. He's said it before: "These kids are so lost and they confuse too many aesthetics. They want it all." You told him he didn't *know* the hosts like you did and that aesthetics are different in California and that maybe what's "confused" in London is "total clarity" in the Bay.

"They get As in computer science," you said. "That's just Berkeley though, everyone gets As." You gave him the look and said, "You study religion, come on."

Your first night here you and Isaac went on a walk and stumbled into an unlocked tennis court. Isaac sat down on the wall and a raccoon ran across the Astroturf – a grey blend of black and white. You began to tear up because you'd never seen one before, and because you were here in America together. Isaac pulled you between his legs and lifted your shirt to kiss your stomach. Eleven hours at thirty-six thousand feet and eight hours on the sun-clock from everyone you knew and loved except each other. Mutually excited and culture-shocked, and it worked like that for six more months. And then one day Isaac woke up panicked, sweating from his temples even though it was January, and showing up late to every class. Because he'd jumped straight from his ex-girlfriend to you. Because he'd never been single and missed out on being selfish. Because he didn't know anything anymore. Because this was supposed to be the year he worked it all out.

After a few weeks of restless nights you thought it might help to take Isaac to this stonemasonry bench. He'd wanted to see it for a while now. He said he'd like to understand its appeal and thrill and calming effect. You warned him he might never understand it because not everyone finds the same things appealing and thrilling and calming – "Like, I find *you* calming but you probably don't find *yourself* as calming." You sat on the bench together in the pseudo-Mediterranean shade and he told you that he did understand it's appeal and that you *were* this bench for him, but that he wasn't sure he should let you be everything in America for him. When you stopped crying he held your face in his hands and said gently, "We're supposed to change here, aren't we?" You told him that you're not changing because you don't think you need to right now, and he said, "You know who you are, though. This scene, it's yours not mine. You've had a million boys and you know you want me." "Don't *you* want *me*?" "Of course I want you, but I want to *know* it." "You need a million girls to know it?" "No, I need myself to know it. I think you forget I've never been alone." "Let's take a break, then," you said.

Josh emerges from his bedroom and you turn to Isaac and say, "Oh, Josh woke up," and then you avert your eyes to the incense that's back in the crack. You kissed Josh two weeks ago – during the break – and Isaac doesn't know. Isaac hasn't been with anyone; when you asked he said the break wasn't about that. After you made Isaac feel dumb for having been worried about Mowgli, he seemed to rule out that whole house as a source of jealousy. You think he thought you were above it. You think you thought so too.

The house is on Ridge Road, on the north side of campus. Only six boys legally live in it – Mowgli, Josh, and four others – although many more pretend to. They met in dorms first year, bonded over music, drugs, and David Foster Wallace. When Mowgli sent you your first Ridge Road invite, the message came from "Savior Sam", because that's how you'd saved his number in your phone the night you met on the grass. You brought a pretty English friend with you because you thought this was the most welcome breed of guest. Isaac was in Santa Cruz on some photography retreat: he'd recently decided to use his camera again. You and your friend decided it was nice to see a house because you thought Berkeley was only frats, sports houses, and co-ops. "The mass-communal living thing really fucks Americans over," she said as you poured another drink in the kitchen, "in England we play house soon as we get to u ni and come out knowing how to coexist with the opposite sex and peel courgettes." You left her with a drunk Mowgli and spent most of your night talking to Josh. He's from Seattle and studies Computer Science. He really seemed to know what he wanted. He took some drug and told you that hearing you speak was like listening to a post-ironic parody of itself, and that it was joyful and bizarre. You didn't know if it was the Computer Science or the dimples, but you talked about him the whole way home.

The next weekend it was your roommate's birthday and the weekend after that you brought Isaac with you to Ridge Road for the first time. When you walked in he took a deep breath, eyes wide. You knew coming here would make him feel like you had something he didn't, but you wanted him to see it anyway. Isaac started talking to some boy he recognized from his Buddhism in Contemporary Culture class so you went to sit with Mowgli. "So *that's* the famous Isaac," he said in an accent that made you feel like a tourist, "you're a pretty couple." You laughed without sound and asked him how you went six months without finding the Ridge Road house. "I feel good here," you said, "it reminds me of home." He put a hand on your thigh and you gently removed it. Mowgli's real name is Sam but his hair is long and greasy and he's often wearing no shirt. Isaac thought you were sitting a little too close to him so he came over and whispered, "I might go," and you stood up and said "Why?" even though you knew, and he muttered, "Can't be fucked with this jungle club shit." You left with Isaac because identity crisis or not you still loved him. On the walk home he said, "I leave you for one weekend and you become a scene girl. Don't you have enough of it at home? This is your year abroad." When his bad mood fell a little you rolled your eyes and said, "Can't believe you were jealous of Mowgli, I picked him up on the grass, the kid's a mess." And between you, the name stuck.

You spent Spring Break with the girls. You didn't pack mascara. They asked about Isaac and you told them the break wouldn't hold. "What's the deal though? You guys don't have real trust issues and you're so invested." "It's bigger than that," you told them, "It just needs time." Patronizing your friends became a first-level coping mechanism – explaining it to them in un-abstract terms would make it too real. You did Beverly Hills and West Hollywood and Malibu and Muscle Beach and all the canyons and galleries and after a few days in LA you felt comfortable enough to change clothes in the street. On the way back to Berkeley you took the Pacific Coast Highway and it was a totally different story to Route 5. You didn't let yourself sleep at all. You pulled over in Santa Barbara to watch the sunset and flick your eyes between the sun, pelicans and dolphins. You're from London so it was completely overwhelming. Your roommate put an arm around you when she saw your eyes water – "It's gonna be okay," she said, "he loves you." When you started driving again the sun had gone and you got out your phone to tell Isaac you needed him but stopped yourself just in time.

You knew you couldn't rely solely on your friends to take you out of this Isaac-withdrawal-low and that's why you kissed Josh. He picked you up and drove you to this magazine launch. Afterwards you went back to Ridge Road and kissed him against the door – it felt strange. His lips, his smell, it kind of turned you on but it wasn't what you wanted when you opened your eyes. You told him you had to pee. When you got home your roommate was awake and asked, "Josh? Which one is that?" "Computer Science," you said. "Jesus, tell Religious Studies *that*."

A few days passed and then you and Isaac talked and talked and talked – in your room, in the lobby, on the Casa Zimbabwe roof, under the bridge, on campus, off campus, and on most Berkeley benches. You didn't tell him about Josh because it was so irrelevant. "I don't wanna be some rebound thing," Josh had said when he called you the next day. "Are you done with Isaac?" Your voice started to choke up because it was kind of the default these days and also because you thought it was easier than saying "obviously no."

Josh raises his chin and waves to you on the couch before he goes to sit with some blonde girl. He looks really good even though he just woke up. His dimples are still prominent and his eyes are still turquoise. You remember him telling you he didn't do blondes. Isaac barely acknowledges the wave. You're not totally sure how you feel about Isaac's oblivion. You think you hate it because it just makes you a little less in sync. The incense stick is still burning, it's getting shorter by the minute. From the corner of your eye you can see Josh sharing a cigarette with the blonde girl.

On one of the benches with Isaac the conversation went like this: "So, who the fuck *is* Isaac?" And then, "No one else can make me as happy but also no one else can make me as sad." You read him the list of everything you've wanted to tell him during the break. "It doesn't make sense not seeing you every day." "I know." "Let's find out who we are together, please." "Okay." It doesn't matter who says what, the sentiment is the same.

The incense is out. Mowgli is trying to sing along to Caribou. You turn to Isaac who's taking a bong hit and whisper, "Where are we?" He puts down the bong and looks around him. "Let's get the fuck out." You sneak away, leaving the Ridge Road residents with the pretenders. He takes your hand and you run all the way from Northside to Southside. He takes you to Strawberry Canyon and jumps the fence to open it from the inside. You walk in. You told Isaac you wanted to skinny dip in a pool while you were in California. "Oh my God," you say. He takes off his clothes and jumps in. You do the same. "I'm not having sex with you," you joke. It's warm and dark and the sky is full of stars. You do a lap and then you swim to Isaac in the shallow end. He pulls you onto him and you run your fingers through his thick black hair. He starts to laugh. "What are you thinking?" you ask. "I've been waiting for something to change. There were no forest fires or police raids. I didn't even feel an earthquake." "That's good," you say. "I know that now," he says, "it took a while but I know that now." "Chill," you say, "West Coast mentality." He's still laughing. You look up at the stars and then back at Isaac. You raise both eyebrows and say, "California dreaming, eh?" He kisses you and says, "I wouldn't go home if you weren't coming with me." You kiss him back and smile. Then you disappear underwater and hold your breath for as long as you can.

HARRIET AVERY

THERE WAS A SILENCE

THE LIGHT SHUNTED ACROSS THE SURFACE OF MY EYES as Jenny guided me the twenty-one steps along the silent platform, the pale needling gleam broken by consistent shadows. I felt an insistent breeze brush over my scalp, tugging at my coat with wicked intent, pulling towards the smell of coffee which was seeping from the café. Our footfalls were all that sounded in the shivering quiet – and then, in the hollow of the silence, a sudden fluttering broke overhead.

I stopped, and felt Jenny stop too, her arm in mine.

'What can you hear?' she said.

I listened to the clapping, fluttering sound, and, for a moment, I was in the past – a seaside holiday, when, one bright morning, the beach was unexpectedly empty, and I could run across its broad expanse like I had never run before, the sand compact and wet beneath my bare feet, the wind streaming past, and gulls rising in thousands around me.

'Just a bird,' I said, pulling myself back into the present with an effort. 'Now, weren't you going to buy a paper?'

She was doubtful. 'I don't have to – it's not important –'

'Oh, go on – I'll be fine!' I told her. 'Just tell me where the waiting room is. I can find my way.'

'If you're sure you'll be okay...' Her voice was lost in the oncoming roar of a train. I felt her hand press mine, and then her grip slipped away. I stood still in the enveloping noise, feeling the rush of displaced air. A high clear whistle blew, and, all at once, the train plunged into the station, roaring and snorting and screaming. The wind encased me with the smell and taste of metal, as the train came to a shuddering stop and the doors grunted open. I was caught in a stream of movement, brushing in all directions, snatches of conversation trailing. From a speaker somewhere above me, a recorded announcement began spooling out a list of stations – *Harling Road, Eccles Road, Attleborough, Spooner Row, Wynondham. For a punctual departure, passengers are asked to close all doors and windows behind them.* Almost immediately, it seemed, the whistle squealed again from the other side of the station; the doors slammed; the engine hum swelled like a balloon. Then, with a sound like rushing water, the train heaved its bulk back into the rhythm of movement. With each clunk of wheel over rail, bars of sunlight played across my face, a momentary lightening against the dull shadows which slipped past like pouring cream.

In the descending quiet, I found my way into the waiting room, feeling my way through the door and letting it close behind me. Emptiness hung in the air. I sat down and remembered immediately what I had thought the last time we had taken this journey: the benches at Thetford station managed to be quite remarkably uncomfortable. There was no position at which the seat remained flat and level.

I shuffled in the silence. Against my spine, the aged wood of the bench held a dull coldness within its knots and grain. I closed my eyes and prepared for a long wait, tasting the dust hanging in space. Outside, the world seemed to have been muffled entirely. No trains roared by. No one entered. It was as if night had fallen unexpectedly in the middle of the day.

Then, there was a sudden thump; the door had apparently crashed into the wall. But it had not swung of its own accord: I could hear the sound of panting from the doorway. Someone had arrived.

I waited, but whoever it was did not sit down. At length, I smiled uncertainly. 'Hello?'

There was a silence. Then the door was shut, the handle creaking as it turned.

'Hello,' a voice said. It was a man, his voice sounding foreign to my ear.

'Waiting for a train?' I asked. 'Perhaps we're getting the same one –'

'I doubt it,' he said. Rather than sitting down, he began to pace back and forth. I felt his agitation moving in the room.

'I expect it will arrive soon,' I said, thinking it might reassure him.

'What?'

'Your train. I assume it's delayed.'

'Delayed – everything is delayed today.'

He seemed to be upset. I didn't know what to do. I grasped the edge of the bench. Underneath the seat, I could feel rivulets of smooth bumps, paint-drips which had begun to form but dried before they could fall.

I listened to him pacing and muttering to himself. I realised I recognised his accent. It reminded me of a young lady called Edyta, who used to sing songs that sounded as if they were being wound backwards. Edyta had looked after me for a few months when Jenny's mother had fallen ill.

'Is... is that a Polish accent by any chance?' I asked.

He paused and then continued to pace. 'Yes, I come from Poland.'

I smiled. 'I have always wanted to go to Poland,' I said. 'Do you miss it?'

'No. It is cold and grey.'

I laughed. 'That's what people say about England.'

'It's the same everywhere.'

'Oh, I don't know about that. Have you ever been to Marseille? It certainly isn't cold there – a friend of mine once told me that the cobblestones get baking-hot, like they've been in an oven.'

'I don't remember France.' he said.

'You've been then?'

'Paris. Long time past.'

He stopped suddenly. A thunderous silence fell. 'You got a wife? And kids?' he asked. Something in his tone had changed.

'Ah, no,' I said. 'I've got my carer, though – Jenny. She's a good girl.'

'Jenny...' he repeated. Something about the way he spoke made me think that he was balancing something fragile with extreme care on the very tips of his fingers. I wondered if there was a window. Maybe he could see something outside.

The silence stretched. I shifted my position. 'Sorry – is everything okay?' I asked.

Then, abruptly, he was sitting next to me. His physical bulk was less than I expected; the fabric of his clothes brushed my arm. He smelt of smoke, and something else, something higher and sweeter. His hand gripped the seat, just as my hand was. I felt the skin of his little finger against my own, the bone of his knuckle. His hand was cold.

I wondered if he wasn't used to British public transport. Maybe he was younger than I had thought. I hesitated. 'Can I ask if you're waiting for someone?'

His response was hidden under a sigh. It almost sounded like, 'I will be,' but something in his tone made me think I must have misheard. I felt the muscles under his skin contract, as if his hand was tightening.

I didn't know what to say. Before I could ask him to repeat what he said, he suddenly spoke as if to change the subject: 'I was in Paris when I was young,' he said. 'With my school. We went to the art gallery.'

'The Louvre?'

'You have been?'

I smiled, and explained that art galleries and I did not really get on.

'It was not that good anyway. Saw the Mona Lisa.' His voice seemed to be tipping backwards and forwards. 'On my wall, in my house, we have a painting. It is of the sea, a very big, wide picture. I look at it sometimes before I go to bed, so that I can dream I'm back in Kolobrzeg, on the sand, with the lighthouse behind.'

Something in what he said caught me unawares and hooked me back into the past, back to that childhood day at the seaside. I felt myself reliving the crunch of the shingle under my feet, and the birds flying before me, as if they were going to drag me up with them, into the clouds, on and on and on.

'But why dream about Kolobrzeg? It's stupid...' His voice fell away.

'I dream about the sea sometimes.' I said, surprising myself. The words seemed to have left my tongue before they reached my brain.

'You do? How?' He asked with no trace of embarrassment.

I twisted my fingers together, taking my hand away from where his lay. 'I don't see it. But I know it. It's different to everywhere else, isn't it? When I was a boy, I thought the sea was like – pieces of the sky fallen here on earth. I thought I could go on, and on, for miles and miles. Forever, even. Nothing to stop me, nothing to make me fall. Because – for me, being outside is – difficult. But the sea, especially early in the morning...' I stopped. How could I explain the almost unbearable freedom? It was like the final release of a long-held breath.

'I know,' he said simply.

For some reason, I knew he understood. I believed him. The words seemed to exist of their own accord between us.

We sat in silence, and listened to each other's breathing.

At length, the station announcement broke through our quietness, reporting that my train was approaching. I reached for my cane. Where was Jenny? I could feel the rushing, urgent energy of the oncoming train, vibrating the tiles under my feet.

'That's my train,' I said, climbing to my feet. *Three steps to the door, the handle at waist-height, turn to the right to open.* Now, the train was here, louder and louder, the roar expanding in my skull. The brakes shrieked shudderingly.

'Hey!' His voice stopped me. 'Do – do you know the way?' he asked.

'I think I do. I'll manage,' I nodded and smiled at him, declining his offer of help, proffered like a hand outstretched towards me. 'Thanks anyway.' I opened the door, and the noise leapt through like a tiger. 'I hope your train gets here soon!' I shouted over the flood. He may have said something else; I could no longer hear him.

I sat in my kitchen as the warm oven bubbled to my left, and the knife on Jenny's chopping board made clear, crisp cuts, dissecting neatly between the tick-tock from the clock on the wall. The hissing smell of the onions frying was so tangible in the room, I felt I could reach out and take hold of it, sticky and warm and loud and sweet.

Jenny had turned the TV on, but muted, so that she could glance at the images, while I listened to the brisk sounds of cooking. But then, with an exclamation, she turned up the volume. I listened in growing horror.

'Our main headline again. Gunman Pawel Krawiec has yet to be captured after killing his wife, and several other members of the public in attacks that are being described as "random and unmotivated". Pawel Krawiec, described as "armed and highly dangerous", has yet to be captured, but police believe him to be still in the Thetford area.'

I felt a shock pulse through me. 'Thetford?'

Before Jenny could answer, the report continued. 'This CCTV footage shows Krawiec moving through Thetford railway station at twelve o'clock today. The police are appealing for any information on his whereabouts or intentions, although residents of Thetford have been warned to remain indoors and not to approach him.'

'Well!' With a click, Jenny turned the TV off. 'All I can say is: I hope they find him quickly.' I could tell she was shaken. Her knife chopped a quick, shocked tattoo on the cutting board.

I sat feeling like I had just been plunged into cold water. 'But I had no idea,' I said, half to myself. 'Why would he have done something like that?'

'Because he's attention-seeking and sadistic,' Jenny spoke with a grimness that was uncharacteristic of her. 'Just like all of the rest of them.'

I could have argued with her, but I didn't. I was silent, as she gave the onions a stir. The vicious whoosh of burning oil sounded like a flame leaping into the darkness, a hand reaching out. A crash of a wave onto shingle.

Of course, Jenny never asked me if I had seen him, and I did not say anything.

AMBERGRIS

DAD CUT OFF HIS PONYTAIL and chucked it into the food bin. I suppose that is the bin it would go in, if I had to guess. Organic matter and all. Recycling. But Mum scooped it out and put it into a little pouch, brushing off the egg shells.

I don't really know why she did that. It's just hair isn't it? But he's been growing it since before I was born.

That hair is older than you, Mum says.

Then it wasn't a very intelligent thing to do was it?

I didn't want to say that to her though. She was curled on the sofa like a Siamese cat, her narrow face the colour of water when you boil beetroots. A face which had been tittering on the edge of the ceramic toilet bowl all morning. Her hair still smelt faintly of vomit and floral perfume. Hair the colour of white gold from years of peroxide and Indian sunbeams.

Isn't hair just dead cells anyway? So really all he did was cut some of the dead cells off his head? Brown dead cells, which are so much older than me that they're dead.

Doctors always warn people about going out in the sun too long. Mum thinks she knows better, she says it's good for my skin. My skin, the spots, the pus, and the "imperfections". On the acne gel bottles they always say TREATS IMPERFECTIONS.

Like I didn't already know my face wasn't perfect. It never does anyway, treat the imperfections.

She won't let me wear makeup, I know some of the other girls do but she tells me to go into the sun. Mum will become leathery like an old crocodile if she isn't careful.

The scissors are stuck in the kitchen table. Dad must have it stabbed last night. I hated that crappy Ikea table anyway. I always had to wipe it down after dinner and it never came up completely clean from the red wine stains. Perfectly round ruby circles, sinking into the chipboard. The scissors were in the middle of it this morning surrounded by bits of glass and sticky patches. The odd strand of hair too.

I imagine it would've taken quite some cutting with those scissors to get through all his hair. They were really blunt from being used to cut the plants. Couldn't he have gone to the bathroom and grabbed the hair scissors? Mum always told him not to use the kitchen scissors on plants.

She told me when I got up this morning. Your Dad got drunk last night and cut off his ponytail. Her cat eyes staring. What did she expect me to say?

I asked if he was bald now or what? I don't know why, as it isn't like he sheared himself like a sheep. But I've never seen him with short hair before. That hair is 25 years old. 10 whole years older than me.

What is she going to do with all that ancient hair anyway? Put it on some sort of altar with incense and my milk teeth she stole when pretending to be the tooth fairy?

I knew already, when I woke up, what he'd done. They don't realize the walls aren't very thick. I could hear them talking, laughing and then listening to some shit old music. Bob Dylan or whatever. Then they started arguing about something. Something about India. Something about how he didn't feel any peace and love anymore. Something about how he couldn't even do yoga in this shit little apartment.

It didn't even sound that great anyway, India. I've seen all the pictures. When they were both young and Mum was more of a kitten than a cat and Dad's skin was glowing orange from way too much sun. The big motorbike was the best bit. But when I ask them about it they tell me I can't ever ride one. Hypocrites.

I wouldn't want to go travelling around bloody India on a bloody motorbike and becoming orange anyway. Let alone wear those beaded dresses Mum was always in.

Some parts of it did look nice though, the beaches and stuff. There are even a few pictures of me, a little worm, lying on the sand all wrapped in a tie-dyed blanket.

I bet it was hot there, but I don't remember the heat.

There are even ones of Mum when she was pregnant, fat as a whale, wallowing in clear water. She was orange even when I was inside her. I wonder if when she vomited back then I could have saved it and sold it as ambergris?

There's a rumbling, fumbling noise coming from their bedroom. It sounds like he might've woken up.

Am I supposed to say anything about his hair?

Mum's ignoring the noise.

He stumbles out and I look up at him. He's like a giant beanstalk with no gold at the top. Only his stupid hair. It's cut in a bob. Not that bad from the front actually.

He walks past me though and I see the back. He looks like a she-wolf. It's all jagged and mangled and dashingly feminine, like he got his hair stuck in a stylish wood chipper.

Christ, my father is an idiot.

MARY BLATCHFORD

DEADLY AMUSEMENT

A thousand gasps in the crowded place shattered the silent amusement
    like a mirror dropped
on a concrete floor. A thousand pairs of eyes stared widely at the
    unmoving pile of a body
sprawled on the wood-chipped floor.

The shadow of the trapeze artist's partner left swinging silently.

Butter fingers.

MEGAN BRADBURY

MOIRA UNLIKELY

THE FIRST TIME I SPOKE TO MOIRA was when she was seven and I was eight. We'd always been in the same class but had never been friends. We were seated alphabetically in those days, and who you sat next to played a big part in who your friends were; my surname began with a B, which meant my best friend was Kathleen Brady, who once made me cry because she called me a fish. I don't know who Moira sat next to.

It was the end of playtime, and we were lining up to go inside for Mass, when I spotted Moira crouched down by the sycamore trees in the corner of the playground. I knew she'd be in trouble if she missed Mass, so I broke away from the rest of the class and ran over to her. I'm fairly certain I only did this because I wanted to be Mary in the nativity that year, and it seemed like the sort of thing the future Mother of Christ might do.

Moira was sifting through piles of fallen leaves. She wasn't wearing gloves, and her hands were mottled with cold.

'Moira,' I said. 'It's time to go in.'

Moira selected a leaf, and positioned it in the strange patchwork of foliage beside her.

'What are you doing?' I asked.

'Making the leaves tessellate,' she said without looking up.

I was used to Moira using words I didn't understand – the other girls were always mocking her for it – but this wasn't one I recognised. 'Tessellate?'

'It means making them fit together,' she explained. 'Here, I'll show you.'

Mass forgotten, I knelt down next to her, watching, fascinated, as she demonstrated how to slot the leaves together like a jigsaw puzzle.

'That's my secret,' she said once she was done. 'Now tell me yours.'

I considered this.

'I salute magpies,' I said eventually.

It was something I'd picked up off my grandmother. Every time she saw a lone magpie, she'd salute it and say, 'Magpie, magpie, where is your mate?' to ward off bad luck, she told me. It drove my mother to distraction – she muttered about this being what you got for marrying into a family of pagans, by which she meant that my father's family didn't go to church every Sunday like we did – so I made sure not to do it when she was around.

I didn't get to hear what Moira thought of this, because we were interrupted by Sister Moses, furious with us for not coming inside when we were told. She shouted at us (I cried; Moira didn't) and sent letters home to our parents. I never got to be Mary in the nativity, and I always suspected that was why; perhaps because of this, I didn't speak to Moira again until secondary school, when she was eleven and I was twelve.

It was during an R.S. lesson; Moira was reading from her essay, which she'd opened with: '"What profiteth a man if he gaineth the world but loseth his soul?" The answer, as anyone with even a basic understanding of mathematics will tell you, is of course one world.' The teacher took exception to this, and sent her to stand in the corridor.

I still have trouble understanding why I did what I did next. Unlike Moira, I wasn't and never have been the sort of person who challenges those in authority. Yet somehow, I found myself standing up and saying to the teacher, 'That isn't fair. She was just expressing her opinion.' Unsurprisingly, the teacher sent me out too, the first and only time that happened.

Out in the corridor, Moira regarded me. 'Why is it you get into trouble every time you try to help me?'

I shrugged.

'It seems pretty unfortunate,' she continued. 'And I thought you had strategies for warding off bad luck.' I frowned, confused, and she added, 'You still salute magpies, right?'

I was stunned. I couldn't believe she'd remembered.

Then she smiled at me, and I smiled back.

'Yes,' I said. 'I do.'

I've no recollection of abandoning my other friends, but I must've done, because from then on, it was always just Moira and I. Even so, it wasn't until a year later that Moira invited me back home, and I discovered her real secret.

Moira lived in a church.

When she'd told me the address, I'd assumed she meant the vicarage. It was in an obscure village just outside the town where we went to school, one I'd seen on a map but never visited; we had to take a bus to get there, and walk for fifteen minutes down narrow country lanes. I felt like I'd stumbled into a story, a feeling which intensified as Moira lead me through the graveyard and into the church.

The strangest thing was, it still *looked* like a church, albeit one with deliberate mistakes. Some of the pews had been arranged to make a living room; there was laundry hanging in the pulpit; the vestry had been converted into a kitchen. The altar and the crucifix were still in place, but I avoided looking at them; they made me feel off-balance.

A girl's head appeared from among the pews. Moira indicated to her. 'Carolyn, this is my sister, Alice. Alice, this is Carolyn.'

Alice scrutinised me. 'With a Y or an I?'

Moira answered before I could. 'Y, no E.'

Alice contemplated this. 'Twelve,' she said, before disappearing back between the pews.

I turned to Moira. 'Twelve?'

'It's how many points your name is worth in Scrabble.'

'I thought you couldn't use proper names?'

'Try telling her that.' Moira was watching me closely. 'Go on. Out with it.'

'What?'

'Well, I don't know if you'd noticed, but this isn't exactly a three-bed semi. You must have theories. Let's hear them.'

I looked around for clues. 'You're...homeless?'

'*Non.*'

'You're ghosts?'

She rolled her eyes. 'Guess again.'

'Err...you're just *really* devout?'

'Now wouldn't *that* be something!' She grinned. 'Come on! There's something I want to show you!'

The *something* turned out to be a large stone angel, hanging up in Moira's bedroom. I'd seen similar statues at my family's church, but there was something wrong with this one. The stone was blackened, and half of the angel's face had crumbled away. Its remaining eye stared down at us balefully.

'There was a fire,' Moira explained. 'Thirteen years ago. The church couldn't afford the repairs, so my dad bought it and moved us in here.'

'Why?'

She shrugged. 'He doesn't live here. He works at a bank in London. I never see him.'

I thought of a church at night, how deep the shadows were, and shuddered. 'Is it just you and your sister?'

No. There was Moira's mother, an academic who spent her time in her office, up in the tower among the bells, writing books no one read about medieval architecture. Moira's brother lived there too, but he was in the Air Cadets and rarely home.

Absent parents. A missing brother. Little to no social interaction at school. Yet Moira seemed content with the situation.

'Don't you get lonely?' I asked as she walked me back to the bus stop.

'One is never alone when one is with the Lord, Carolyn.' Moira managed to maintain a serious expression for about five seconds before bursting into laughter. I laughed too, but I noticed she didn't answer my question.

When I got home, I told my family all about it. My mother pursed her lips and said they seemed 'an unlikely family'; my sister Cecily misunderstood thus, taking 'unlikely' to be Moira's surname. 'Are you going to the Unlikelys?' she'd asked me, which my father found hysterical. He was the one who coined the nickname, Moira Unlikely, and insisted on using it for the duration of our friendship.

Unlikely wasn't the only name Moira made for herself. Her insubordination hadn't gone unnoticed; once the story about the church got around (something I sensed my mother had a hand in) she became everyone's favourite topic for gossip, and the more they talked, the more she acted up. 'They seem to enjoy disapproving of me,' she explained. 'It'd be a shame to deprive them.'

Moira had a point. People weren't interested in the Moira who once treated me to a daytrip to Lyme Regis after she found out I'd never been to the seaside. They preferred to discuss the Moira who was excluded for breaking into school and putting Santa hats on all the Virgin Mary statues. My involvement in this scheme was never referred to, because no one knew about it; Moira insisted on taking the blame. 'I want a partner in crime,' she said. 'Not a partner in punishment.'

Shortly after this incident, I overheard Cecily asking my mother, 'If Moira lives in church, does that mean she's definitely going to heaven?'

'It doesn't work like that,' my mother replied, before changing the subject. She'd always been suspicious of Moira, and the stories confirmed what she'd already surmised: Moira would be a Good Girl Gone Bad, the sort who rolled up their skirts and tied their ties around their thighs like garters, who hung around in the park with alcohol and cigarettes and boys, who dropped out of school at sixteen because they'd *got into trouble*. She didn't understand. Moira wasn't like that. She was something new.

'What would you say,' Moira asked me once, 'if you knew that tomorrow, no one would remember what you'd said?' We were lying on our backs in the graveyard, staring up at the sky.

'I'd tell my mother I don't believe in God.'

'Don't you?'

'I just want to know how she'd react.'

'And your dad? What would you tell him?'

'That combing his hair over his bald patch like that isn't fooling anyone.' I pulled myself up onto my elbows. 'What about you?'

She smirked. 'I'm with you about the bald patch.'

I laughed. 'No! I mean, what would *you* say? That you don't believe in God?' Moira stayed silent. 'You don't, do you?'

'I'm open to the possibility.'

'But at school...you're so...'

'That's different! I don't approve of being told what to do. It reduces people to sheep.'

'I do what I'm told,' I teased. 'Does that make *me* a sheep?'

'I prefer to think of you as the lost lamb in the parable.' She rolled over onto her stomach. 'Everyone knows that in the end, the shepherd will find you and return you to the flock, but you can still have a fine time with me while it lasts.'

Most people expect this story to end badly, but it doesn't, not really. We just drifted apart, as friends who essentially have little in common often do. After leaving school, I moved away and we lost contact; I didn't see Moira again until twenty-four years later, when she was forty-two and I was forty-three.

We passed one another in the street, when I was in town visiting my parents. Moira looked older and more tired. We exchanged stilted comments about how it'd been; then I said I had to be somewhere and I'd best be on my way. As I turned to go, she asked if I still saluted magpies. I told her I didn't.

That evening, I asked my father if he knew what'd happened to Moira.

He was taken aback. 'Moira Unlikely? It's been years since you've mentioned her.'

It turned out Moira still lived in the area. She'd been married twice, divorced once; she had two children and worked as a teacher at a local school.

'It's not the life you'd have predicted for her, is it?' my father said when he'd finished.

I said nothing. I couldn't decide if I was disappointed or not. I didn't know what I'd been expecting of her, but I knew it was more than that.

But then, that was Moira, I suppose. Unlikely to the last.

RHIANNON BUTLIN

ORCHARD BEACH:
A SERIES OF PORTRAITS

I T IS ALMOST IMPERCEPTIBLE, beginning when the spring rots into
summer and the plump fruit that lined the boughs now sits at the
roots, fermenting into a sweet spicy liquor that sends the seagulls looping
though the air. The people of The Bronx leave the dirty heat of New York
for Orchard Beach.

*

*Sweating bodies pile into subway carriages. Mom ushers them in, shamelessly
yelling instructions, in a way only Mothers can. She sits herself down with her
youngest on her lap, her oldest sitting beside her and Maria before her. The
train pulls away from the station and she hooks her finger into Maria's belt
loop to steady her. The little girl holds a rolled up towel purposefully under
her arm. From the other arm hangs a plastic grocery bag. Inside, white-
bread sandwiches, home-made sunscreen, iodine and baby oil and brightly
coloured juice boxes upon which hosts of smiling animals congregate. Maria
likes animals. Every so often she swings her head, making her little pink hair
bobbles clatter together.*

*

Jamaica, where barefoot boys with soft muscles and hard feet skirt the
tide, chewing on sugar cane, or holler to sailors for odd jobs far beyond
their physical capability which they stoically attempt a few times before
collapsing on the ground in fits of giggles. The tide swells against the
shore like it has since the beginning of time and tall limber palm trees

submit to the breeze, curving their spines languorously. Only the disorder of man could interrupt the soft inhalation-exhalation of the land.

The war came in 1939 and the men left, chasing stolen pictures, in flickering black and white, of boyhood adventure and 1886 rifles. Gone with the tide, and with them, the music. Back then, the bands that played at weddings, baptisms and other town gatherings would consist of a gaggle of men somewhere between sixteen and thirty years old. They packed up that music in bags and suitcases, tucked it into pockets. The stillness came and the soft-muscled, hard-footed boy was left sat slumped on the sand, the sugar cane hanging limply out of his mouth.

*

He stands outside the apartment building throwing bits of gravel at the window, Paulo's cheesy like that, Tiffany thought to herself. She leans her head out, her hair falling forward and yells down, 'shut up you asshole, you'll wake my mom!', but she's giggling. They break into a run down the sidewalk, in case they miss them, her always running a little ahead and looking back to laugh. 'Eh! Eh! We're here.' They clamber into the convertible, shined up last night, two in the front, three in the back. Her perched on Paulo's lap. Hiked-up skirts, naked thighs, paper-bagged glass bottles, and him, thanking God for every bump and swerve in the road, and her, with a devilish look in her eye that he wouldn't know until he was a little older.

*

And so, that soft-muscled, hard-footed boy grew a little older and found a girl who felt like home. He borrowed a suit and bought a pair of scarlet coloured suede shoes and her mother altered her wedding dress, a little shorter, a little fuller, and they were married in a chapel by the sea. And when they had left, the birds ate the rice and all was as it was and ever had been again and days became weeks became months.

*

The morning rises and spins into noon and the children return to where their families congregate beneath umbrellas for melted chocolate bars and potato chips. Only a few young stragglers are left, darting and skipping along the shore, dodging her as she walks slowly up and down the beach. None of the children know Lady and yet each and every one of them unconsciously but unquestionably treats her with an inexplicable deference. Her black bikini is laced with brown leather cord, her parasol is of a matching brown and rests upon her shoulder like a halo. Among the jewelled trash and candy-coloured bikes she is the cool wet earth beneath the shadow of the tree. Her Mother, sitting further up on a plastic garden chair, turns to her sisters and says 'Oh isn't Lady a funny one' but children just have a way of knowing.

*

That was until he came home one night with fizzing, wild eyes. She finally slammed her hand down on the kitchen table. 'What! What then! Out with it!' And he did, like a guilt-ridden and apologetic young child he spilled out his dreams. And she was raised up right wasn't she, and she'd taken those vows hadn't she? Till death do us part. So she followed him, just like those young men before them, out with the tide.

*

As the sun edges further towards the horizon, the Taylor children begin to tire, one by one abandoning sand-castles, or sand-igloos or other indistinguishable sand-constructions. Until each one sits cross legged in the semi-circle around Gramma in patient anticipation. Even the youngest know there's no use in rushing her. A few minutes pass until she cracks open one almond kernel eyelid. 'Now, you all know that 'fore I had your Momma I lived down in Atlantic City,' she begins slowly, 'now down there they got a beach, lot like this one, whites first ones to call it Chicken Bone Beach in the beginning I think, anyway, soons everyone was callin' it that an' no one could remember what its real name was to begin with, well they called it that cos sure enough, whole beach lined with chicken bones, height o' summer it was pretty dangerous, kids running round with no shoes on, getting themselves cut up, place half swarming with gulls, fighting for scraps. Now these white folk would walk on past the beach shaking their heads, used to say it was cos negro folk so dirty, leavin' they trash about like that, they's animals, they'd say, and it'd sure seem that way, huh, but you ever go to a white folk beach and you might notice something' and she opened her mouth just a little and gave a soft cackle, 'sees white folks' beaches had men that'd turn up in the evenin' and pick up all the litter,' 'here, it'd never occurred to us that those white folk had been spreadin just as much trash about, they just had people to clean up after 'em!'

She made a home for them, out the grime and the darkness of Harlem, but the children stood outside, kicking cans and looking perpetually lost.

And then Moses came, and led us all out of Egypt, to the Promised Land.

His name was Robert Moses, a perpetually suited man with sloping eyebrows. In 1947 he slammed his pen down on a city map and the towering grey waves were parted. Whole neighbourhoods were torn aside, replaced by one mile of silver beachfront, made, not by the will of God, but the hand of man.

*

Kevin dug his fingers into the wet sand and looked up at his big brother sitting beside him, a little straighter, a little higher. It had always been this way, in every memory Selassie had towered over him, even after Kevin had started to catch up. Selassie and before that King and before that Jonathan. Selassie had always recognised the malleability of a name, something one could shed like skin. Skin. A quivering flag in green, yellow and red and the profile of Lion upon it. The Letters K and G in unsteady gothic lettering which the brothers shared. Two teardrops, one filled, one unfilled. And Kevin, R.I.P. 1994-2009 inked onto his skin. Selassie sat alone on the sand and looked out before him. His eyes fell upon some indistinguishable piece of humanity, glittering and red, discarded at the mouth of the ocean, swallowed by the froth and carried out with the tide.

*

The Puerto Rican woman next door first told her about it. That Sunday, after church, she had prepared their lunch, packed their towels and they'd travelled out to Orchard Beach. Humans, drawn to the water by some growling prehistoric desire and a more conscious longing that painted the inside of their eyelids in shining aquamarine blue. And so, the people of The Bronx had carved out their own migratory pattern. Not some colonial quest set out upon by men clasping weapons and hunting for gleaming things trapped in rocks, men with money in their eyes and blood on their hands. No, they came like children, led by their soul. Noah picked up each of his children, one on either shoulder and walked out, into the tide, and his wife followed.

JULIAN CANLAS

TRISTAN AND HIS MUM'S VOYAGE TO THE GREAT ELSEWHERE

Mum and I left dad's house in fire when I was nine,
in a night barefoot procession of cicada hymns.
The moon had folded itself into a glare,
shrivelling away from the humdrum heat;
the mud solidified on our legs into new
skin, covering us like wine stains; we could see
nothing: not the ripples of the earth,
nor our limbs, nor our path.

TRISTAN AND *LES DAMOISELLES D'AVIGNON*

Cassetta-framed, the five women's stares exist like a sigh,
a slow exhale from the exhibition heat, which has crawled

into my skin. Sweat courses down, stealing bits of dark beige
and reapplying the melanin as paint. The female voice of the audio

guide beckons: 'none of the five women are conventionally attractive.'
The fluorescent light retracts like birth in reverse; I am

in my childhood bedroom lying in my bed on my chest. I am sweating
in the evening heat and trying to understand these same five

angular women, who are captioned nude female prostitutes
in the same space where popes, and geniuses, and women newly

acknowledged are labeled. In this Picasso exhibition, I sit
on a bench, staring at the women and their angular

imperfections, and I can hear the booming laughter of dad
and his mates, as they drink. 'You should sleep,' mum says;

her face, like my bedroom, is a round vacant space,
where no sharpness exists, her workplace pearl necklace

and apron tied tightly around her neck, her wedding ring
staining the off-red scenery beige like the five women's

painted flesh, harsh in the fluorescent lighting of the exhibition.
'The Damoiselles d'Avignon are menacing and angular,'

the female voice says, but that is until they wear mum's face.
The five women capture the spaces into complete stillness.

LOUIS CHESLAW

SINK

"**Y**OU WOULDN'T DO THAT FOR ME AND YOU KNOW IT."
"Neither would he!"
"But I don't know that, do I? That's what you can't seem to understand. It's annoying knowing everything about you, Mark. It's boring." Chloe said all of this while pinning her hair up with chopsticks. It was alluring and, watching her, Mark found himself hoping that his next girlfriend would have a similar skill.

"If I ask you a question, Mark, I know exactly what your response will be, no matter the subject. When I was talking to Alexei tonight, I had no idea what he'd say."

"Alexei? You learnt his name?"

"Of course I did. That's what I'm saying. Before we went out tonight I had no idea that that was his name, and now I do. I learnt something tonight. I knew your name was Mark before we left, so what would have been the point of spending the evening talking to you?'

"What do you mean you didn't know his name before we went out? You didn't even know he existed before we went out!"

"That's precisely my point."

Mark sighed. He'd been watching her all night, from the moment she'd left his side as they'd walked in. His eyes had followed her as she'd greeted friends and colleagues, never once stopping to talk for longer than a minute or so, circling the room as if she were walking along the rim of a glass. She'd alighted at various tables as she went, occasionally leaning in to hear someone, laughing when the moment called for it.

When the time had come for music, social decorum called for her to be restored to him. Dancing, he'd felt her spine through her dress, and was glad to note that she'd lost the weight he'd asked her to. At home now, however, looking at her reflection in the dressing room mirror as she took off her makeup, the transformation was even more apparent. Her cheeks, previously indistinct from the rest of her face, had become framed by salient cheekbones, which in turn seemed to exercise control over the movement of her mouth, like the handles of a marionette.

"If you know so much about him, then why was he there?"

"What do you mean why was he there?"

"Groom or groom?"

"Very funny, Mark. He was a guest of Sam's – they work together. Until this morning he'd never even met Ryan."

Mark knew he was getting testy. He wasn't even sure what he'd sought to get out of the question, other than a confirmation from her that they'd spoken to each other, which he realised now she'd already provided. He'd like to have said that their conversations were like games of chess, but he knew he wasn't – they weren't – smart enough for that analogy to hold true.

Casting his mind back to the party, Mark scrabbled for an anecdote he could use as a retort, something to show that he'd also been able to have an interesting, spontaneous conversation with someone. He was struggling, however, to remember what he'd spent his evening doing. He and Chloe had been seated next to each other at dinner, which accounted for one hour of the two-and-a-half, but that still left ninety minutes. Ninety minutes that had been ample time for his girlfriend of eight months to learn Alexei's name.

He'd spoken to Alissa, but only because she'd initiated a conversation to try to ascertain Chloe's whereabouts, before informing Mark that, yes, she "definitely could fall in love" with someone or other, but that "he's just not given me enough to fall in love with yet," answering a question Mark couldn't remember having asked in the first place.

He recalled at one point also receiving a lecture of sorts in the bathroom from Zach Lennon, who always seemed to be chewing his cheeks as he spoke: "I don't even need to be in here, but if your date says she needs the bathroom, wherever you are, you do too. It's a win-win, bro. She gets to feel less weird about going, and you get to maintain the balance of power, you know?" Zach had a habit of speaking to you as if he were actually talking to someone just over your shoulder. "You aren't waiting around, looking like a little nobody in her eyes while she powders her nose for the next guy."

Yet apart from these two, thankfully brief encounters, those ninety minutes were something of a blur. With that, he returned his focus to the present moment.

"What do you want to do tonight?"

"Go to bed? It's two in the morning."

"So? I bet Sam and Ryan aren't going to sleep yet."

"They're newlyweds, Mark. I'd hope for their sake that they weren't."

He placed his hand on the back of her chair, and kissed her shoulder. As quickly as he'd returned to a standing position, Chloe had found a hand towel, using it to wipe his kiss away. She did the same to her other shoulder in an attempt to appear less conspicuous, and Mark pretended not to have seen either movement.

"Brush your teeth."

Not knowing whether this was just another jibe from Chloe, or perhaps a coital pre-requisite, and not wanting to risk it in case it were the latter, Mark obliged. He approached the sink, picking up his toothbrush. Unable to see the toothpaste, he resolved that as long as he was out of her eye-line she'd be none the wiser. He ran the brush under the tap, bringing it to his mouth as he evaluated himself in the mirror. Bags under his eyes belied the conscientious effort he'd been making to get eight hours of sleep a night, and he wondered whether this was just something that came with breaking twenty-five.

"The toothpaste's over here."

In the time it took for him to spit and try to form a response, Chloe vacated the room. Left alone, Mark took his phone out of his pocket. He'd received no new messages, and so set an alarm for seven the next morning, putting the phone in the sink, after wiping it dry with Chloe's hand towel, to amplify the noise. Leaving, he turned out the dressing and bedroom lights simultaneously, losing his visual on Chloe's silhouette under his sheets as he did so. Night's coat had fallen, and no one would hang it up until morning.

GABY CORRY-MEAD

WHEN THE BLACK CAT CAME TO TEA
OR
THE-EVENING-OF-WHICH-
WE-DO-NOT-SPEAK

ON A SMALL ROAD IN CENTRAL LONDON there is a restaurant where the frequenters of Covent Garden and Leicester Square convene to drink Moet at £20 a glass and indulge in scallops, girolles and pomme purée. Here, however, is not the focus of this telling. Instead, look past the pristine napkins to a place altogether darker. Next to the restaurant is a hunched building, the windows made of small panes and black lattices. It is a place impossible to see when you are looking *at* it, especially impossible if you are looking *for* it, but if you happen to pass it and look out of the corner of your eye you will see, in spidery gold lettering, neatly engraved above the building, a sign that reads:

Messrs Scoff and Banter's Services for the Recently Deceased

It is into this world – this Victorian funeral parlour sitting quite inconspicuously in the second decade of the 21ˢᵗ century – that you must place half your attention, else you will lose it all together. If you half-listen very carefully, you will half-notice that someone is shouting…

'…and furthermore, he's always the first to wash his dainty hands of any and all responsibility. Only this morning I had to promise him a week's worth of cooking before he'd even contemplate doing the shopping for this evening. And even then he still left me to rearrange the furniture, polish, cook, clean – organise the whole bloody thing! And what's more...'

'Enough, Cornelius. You've had your hour.'

Cornelius Banter paused for breath, upset that his hour had been used up already. The grandfather clock struck three o'clock with twelve slow chimes. Today's recipient of Cornelius's tirade was the shop's raven, a formidable-looking thing with sharp black eyes that stared exasperated at Cornelius, who huffed,

'You really are no use at all. It's as if no one cares...'

'Enough!' the raven rasped, his voice like Velcro. 'Scoff will walk through that door any moment and you can tell him about your petty problems.'

Cornelius harrumphed, sank into his armchair, tucked his chin into his thick orange beard and grumbled quietly to himself.

Fortunately for the raven, who prided himself on being one of the few living beings in the shop, no sooner had he mentioned his name than the creak-tinkle of the shop door announced Sebastian Scoff. Scoff was a tall man, thin, with a set of pince-nez delicately balanced on his sharp nose. A slick of iron hair lay neatly coiffed when he removed his top hat and placed it on the wrought iron hat stand. It was exceedingly satisfying for Cornelius, who was, by nature, everything that Scoff was not, to see Scoff bedecked in bright orange shopping bags, a most unflattering set of accessories.

'Good day, Mr Scoff,' muttered Cornelius, digging his fingernails into the armrest.

'Good day, Mr Banter. I trust you have made the appropriate preparations for this evening?'

Cornelius snorted. Of course nothing was ready.

'My dear Banter, you do know I hate it when you mumble like that,' Scoff began, unloading the shopping onto the embalming table. 'Am I to take from your moaning that you have not readied anything? Honestly, it's as if you don't take the Society seriously. I, on the other hand, traversed the length and breadth of town to locate a Waitrose, only to find it closed and with no alternative but to face the indignity of Sainsbury's. Really, Mr Banter, Sainsbury's! I felt so awfully out of place, I'm convinced I've contracted some sort of hideous disease, and the people...'

Were it possible for a man to become feral in the amount of time it took for Scoff to unload the shopping, Cornelius would have been foaming at the mouth by the time he launched himself at his colleague.

As it was, Scoff was knocked to the floor not by a feral creature, but a screeching auburn fuzz in undertaker's clothing. The pair tussled on the ground for a few minutes but, since neither was as young as he once was, inflicted little more than slaps and hair pulling before they got tired, called it a draw and put the kettle on.

Scoff poured the tea into mugs. The handle of one had been fashioned into a penguin and said 'Let's break the ice with a cuppa', the other was black and sported the Iron Maiden logo. Both Scoff and Cornelius admitted the mugs jarred violently with the Victorian macabre of the teapot but the original cups had long since been broken or used to store formaldehyde and they knew better than to go to IKEA again.

'You needn't worry, old chap,' said Scoff, taking a tentative sip. 'Three hours is plenty of time for you to get everything in order. They arrive in dribs and drabs anyhow – lord knows if the Earl will even show.'

The Black Cat, of which Scoff and Banter are proud members, is an elite dining society established by the fourth Duchess of Piccadilly in 1840. Known for its exclusivity, the Black Cat only accepts into its membership Victorian ladies and gentlemen who exist in a blissfully anachronistic state amongst the Kit Kat wrappers of Kentish Town and the smartphones of South Ken. Above all, the Cats pride themselves not only on their lust for fine dining but the lengths they go to in order to make every meal a gastronomical, theatrical, quite sensational experience. Each month, it is the turn of a member to host the Society in their place of residence. The evening must then be themed to that residency in whatever manner the host chooses. Messrs Scoff and Banter, therefore, were going to hold a séance.

After half an hour's rummaging through chest upon chest of brushes, pins and all such paraphernalia needed to stop a corpse from looking and acting like a corpse, Cornelius appeared in the parlour, as red and manic as his beard.

'Whatever is the matter, my dear fellow?' said Scoff, half-glancing up from his fashion pull-out.

Cornelius huffed, his clenched fists shaking. 'I cannot find a single item for this evening; that is the matter. Why is it that whenever I organise something that might actually help us rebuild our frankly laughable reputation, you always spoil it with one of your impractical jokes? I will not stand for it, Scoff.'

Scoff sipped his fourth cup of tea and dispassionately continued reading the article entitled 'Colour by Jumpers: what block colour can do for your figure'. Cornelius seethed quietly by the back of the armchair, letting out the occasional barb such as, 'I should have left when you murdered Houdini,' (Cornelius's beloved pet rabbit who, through entirely unknown circumstances, became Scoff's beloved pet rabbit pie, the name was a painful irony) before Scoff said finally,

'I believe you'll find you laid your inventory on the chest of drawers yesterday morning to save you the trouble of looking for it today.'

At six o'clock the grandfather clock let out another twelve chimes, signalling the arrival of four hungry Cats, the first of whom arrived before the twelfth chime had ended. Baron von Hagerweiss was another tall thin man with a rattish face that always looked uncomfortable, disapproving, or both.

'Good evening,' was all he said.

The Baron hung his hat next to Scoff's, taking care not to let the two touch; he would not have his effects contaminated by the lower orders.

At half past six, the door burst open to reveal what any sane pair of eyes would describe as a walking armchair. Madame Bonneheure, who embraced her name as fully as one can by completely ignoring it, was, and she herself would admit this, a woman who loved her food to the point of becoming it. She was very large and very beautiful and was adored for her 'bubbly personality'; the only person who did not love Bonneheure was the Baron, which only made Mme. Bonneheure's delight in tormenting him with her affections all the greater.

Seven o'clock came and went. Still the table was not full.

Mme. Bonncheure piped up, eyeing the kitchen, 'The rules do state that after an hour, food should be served even if not all members are present.'

'An excellent idea, Madame,' said Scoff with a smirk, 'or at least it would be if we had any food to serve. My esteemed colleague stretched this evening's theme to its limit and carbonised the plum-cake.'

Mme. Bonneheure gasped. 'You mean I have trekked all the way here, in my tightest corset,' she slipped a hand onto the Baron's upper-inner thigh, 'for nothing more than to sit in a dingy funeral parlour? This will not do. I shall take my leave this instant.'

Everyone was too concerned with corsets, upper-inner thighs and plum-cakes to notice the dark figure standing quietly in the doorway.

'Not so fast, ma chérie,' he said, waltzing into the half-light. 'The night is still young, no? And besides, 'er Ladyship 'as been dying to see you.'

There is little to say about the Earl of Brixton, not because he is uninteresting, but because anything said about him will probably be wrong. Some know him as 'the old black guy who busks outside M&S', to others he is the stray cat you think is yours but is being fed by the whole street. He is a law unto himself and that is how he shall stay. That evening, he was Papa Legba, all top hat and dreadlocks, as menacing as any who can control the spirits of the dead, and in the crook of his arm he carried a sleek black cat.

'From both 'er Ladyship and my 'umble self, I bid you good evening.'

'Oh Earl, it is so wonderful to see you,' cried Mme. Bonneheure. 'We were so afraid you would be unable to attend, weren't we Baron?'

The Baron winced as he was kicked under the table. 'Yes.'

Such a commotion had been caused by the arrival of the Earl and her Ladyship – the tenth Duchess of Piccadilly – that the guests had quite forgotten the issue of the plum-cake and, it seemed, the existence of their hosts.

Cornelius cleared his throat. 'Ehem, excuse me everyone. Please, I'd just like...'

'My dear friends,' Scoff interrupted, 'I believe my colleague intends to begin this evening's entertainment. Your cooperation would be deeply appreciated, if only to save us all the trouble of being attacked by my associate. Now, Mr Banter, would you care to lead the evening...'

The séance had not even begun when the problems started. Cornelius returned from the kitchen not with tall white candles appropriate for such an occasion, but an assortment of festive candles because Scoff had forgotten to buy any and the corner shop was shut. The Baron's face as he watched the foot- tall Father Christmas with first degree burns placed in front of him was enough to make Mme. Bonneheure's evening.

Anyone passing by the parlour at such a time probably would not have half-noticed a short, rotund man of unmistakably orange appearance trying to settle an altercation between a very angry Earl and the spirit of a recently deceased bailiff who had evicted the Earl from a squat in Islington the previous year. They might have half-missed the self-same Earl questioning the spirit of a beloved pet rabbit into the identity of its killer; though they might have half-heard the distinctive chink of crockery smashing against a wall, followed by the cry of: 'Rabbit murderer!'

To this very day, if you found Cornelius Banter in a coffee shop around Seven Dials and asked him about what became of the evening on which The Black Cat came to tea, he would not answer you. He would rather take Scoff back to IKEA and have him redesign the shop than discuss The-Evening-Of-Which-We-Do-Not-Speak. As it happens, another trip to IKEA is in order for Messrs Scoff and Banter, something about a new teapot.

JACK DE QUIDT

THE COMBINED MILES

One of the nice things about driving at night is noticing things in the
          windows as you
pass by.
Earlier there was a window and inside the window was a pot plant, some
          sort of spider
plant
Placed perfectly in the centre.
(They remembered a class where they cut a spider plant into little segments
          and each
one grew
And that was symbolic enough for them.)
The room behind it was green and the coach smelled of popcorn
And someone had bought that plant and carried it up two flights of stairs.
That was that house. It took us four seconds to pass it by.

Then there was the Country Style Furniture Shop with the sign saying
          exactly that.
The inside of the shop was dark.
On the outside were the words "closing down" and "everything must go" and
          "fine stock
here"
And someone had hung fairy lights above them, so the Country Style
          Furniture Shop's
failure
Was at least pretty coloured.
What more can we hope for, really?
Someone, string fairy lights above our failed furniture businesses.
That was the store.
It took us a minute to pass by because the coach was stuck in traffic.

And then there was the disused train warehouse
Where the trains would have visited to be serviced and replaced and stored.
Now it was empty, but inside you could have turned on the big white lights and smelled
the paint.
You could have laid on the floor and imagined the weight of the trains above you.
The metal, the combined miles, the passengers holding plastic cups of coffee.
Anyway, that was the train warehouse.
We passed it pretty quickly because it was beside a motorway.

Then finally there was that little terraced house, yellow walls.
I could see an archway between two rooms inside. There was a bead curtain pulled
back.
It was a kitchen of some sort, a dark wood bookshelf on one of the walls. Soft light.
The coach was suddenly filled with the smell of a cheese and tomato pasta bake
And I wanted nothing more, I wanted nothing more
Than to sit down in that room, in the crook of those walls, and eat, and talk, and they'd
Say "how was the day?" and I'd say "long,"
And they'd say "how was your journey," and I'd say
"I'm so glad you're here and this house is here and the crook of these walls."

ANASTASIA DUKAKIS

READY OR NOT

TWO MONTHS AGO GRETA GOT LOST, but then she got finded again.
She got lost on the last hide and seek, the special one where I was the
counter. The other kids in the block didn't want me to play because they
were really big, like eight years old. They always said, 'Eww, Matth-ew's
a baby.' But Greta always said, 'Hey, lay off,' and she's a bigger kid so they
had to say 'Ahh, okay.' I always wanted to be the counter, but normally I
hided with Greta. I wasn't very good, so we always got finded quick. But
Greta never minded, she just smiled and said, 'Hey, we came first from
the back,' which meant we actually lost but it was okay.

On the last hide and seek, I asked Greta if I could be the counter.
I said, 'I got lots of practice counting', which is true. Normally she said
no, but that last time she said yes. I counted one to ten three times, and
then looked in the garden at the back, then at the front bit of the block.
But Greta hided for the longest time ever and we didn't find her for
the whole day.

Greta was so good at hiding that the police went looking for her. I
saw their cars in the car park when Mum took me to school. They had
yellow and blue highlighter squares and 'POLICE' written on the front.
Sometimes when I was at home I heard them go 'whee-oo whee-oo' as
they went past.

Once the police started coming to the block, the posters started
going up. All of them had Greta in a pink T-shirt, and the word 'Missing'
underneath. There were other words too, but Mum never let me look
because she said The Boss wouldn't like it, and The Boss meant big
business so I had to listen. So I just saw the posters from far away, on the
lampposts when we drove to school. Even from far I could see Greta was

smiling happy on them. Sometimes when Mum was late taking me to school she drove really fast, and it looked like Greta's teeth were jumping from one lamppost to the next.

Then a month later everything stopped. The police and the posters disappeared. One night, I even saw Greta on TV.

Mum and me were eating dinner in the living room, with our spaghetti plates on our legs. I was sticking my chin in the spaghetti smoke while Mum watched the weatherman on TV. Then she went out the room, and the TV said, 'And now for the news.'

Greta came on screen, the same Greta from the posters. Next to her was a man, but he was all boxy so I couldn't see his face properly. I was excited because this meant Greta was really famous, on TV famous, so I shouted to Mum, 'Look, it's Greta!' But as soon as she heard me she switched off the TV. I was annoyed.

'Greta got finded,' I said. Mum just breathed like she was about to go under water.

'I want to see where she hided so long,' I said.

But Mum shaked her head and mentioned The Boss, so I ate the rest of my spaghetti quietly. Then I brushed my teeth and Mum gave me my goodnight kiss.

But that night I didn't really stay in bed. I pretended to sleep, then got up and creeped quiet quiet into the bit outside Mum's bedroom. That was where Mum had the night talks with Dad, because he came home late and left early in the morning. That night Mum was already talking when I got to the door:

'They found her, and Matt saw on TV.'

'Jesus woman, what were you doing showing him that? Are you fucking insane?'

'I wasn't trying to – it came on unexpectedly. As soon as I knew I switched it off. I'm sorry.'

Dad did a snorting sound like a horse, then Mum talked more.

'Still, I think he needs to know.'

'Hah. What exactly does Matthew need to know?'

I put my ear closer.

'Well, he needs to know what happened to Greta. The fact that she's–' Mum stopped. She sounded like the words were doing hot potatoes, and she couldn't touch them long.

'Matthew doesn't need to know anything. Don't make this difficult.'

'He should know a little, at least,' Mum said. It was hard for me to hear her voice, it was so small and soft.

'Fuck's sake, do you ever listen? Here's how it is: we tell him nothing, you keep your bloody mouth shut. Case closed.' His voice had gotten louder, like it always did in the night talks.

'No. No, you don't get to– ' Mum said, but then there was a hit sound. That scared me, so I did Mum's rule to count to ten. By the time I got to ten, she would be talking, which meant everything was 'super-duper'. I always used that rule in the night talks. This time I got to nine and then Mum said 'Okay, okay,' which meant things were sort of okay. I heard the door unlock, so I ran back to bed and did pretend sleep until it became real.

The next day Mum said The Boss didn't want me to go to school, so we played doctor instead.

I put my red stethoscope on Mum's shirt, and she made it say 'ba-dum ba-dum', which is the sound hearts make zoomed in. I wanted to continue, but Mum stopped.

'Matt, I have something serious to tell you.'

'Big business?' I said.

'Yeah. This is going to be hard for you, but Greta is gone.'

'TV said Greta got finded,' I said.

Mum didn't say anything for a while. Then she said, 'The TV meant she's sort of gone, but sort of found.'

'Where's she sort of found?' I asked.

'I'll show you,' Mum said.

We went downstairs to the garden. The grass was patchy like old people's hair, with flowers on the edge where the woods began. Mum turned to talk to me.

'Sometimes bad things happen, even if it's unfair. When Greta went into the woods, bad things happened. That's why you must never go there.'

I looked at Mum. I didn't know Greta went into the woods.

'This is big business. Do you understand?'

I nodded.

'You finded Greta?' I reminded Mum.

'Sort of found Greta,' she reminded me.

'Show me where,' I said.

Mum crouched down so we were the same.

'Greta is here,' she said. She put her hand on my T-shirt like her hand was the red stethoscope.

'And here,' she said, putting her hand on her own shirt.

'And there,' she said, pointing to the flowers.

'I don't see her,' I said.

'I know. I wish I could explain better, but I can't. Just remember that Greta may be gone in some ways, but she's still in our hearts.'

I nodded okay, but my brain was zig-zagging. How did Greta get into my heart? How did she fit? When Mum went 'ba-dum ba-dum', was that Greta's heart too?

Later on when Mum was putting the special pink paint on a bruise, I sneaked down to the garden. I shouted 'Greta', and looked around the flowers, but she wasn't there.

For the next few days I looked for Greta, but she was never in the garden, or in my heart. Then I thought: maybe Greta had gone into the woods again. Mum said not to go, but I thought how lonely Greta must be. So I went.

Inside was different than Mum said. There was squelchy mud and splashy puddles. Trees covered the sky, but bits of sunlight came through and made pretty patterns on the floor. As I looked in one puddle, I saw Greta's face smiling next to mine.

'Greta!' I said.

But before I could turn around Mum appeared. She grabbed my hand and started walking home. I said 'ouch' because she was squishing my hand, but she ignored me. As we left Greta shouted, 'See you soon,' but Mum ignored her too.

When we got inside Mum started talking.

'Just what did you think you were doing?'

'Finding Greta,' I said, but Mum was already talking again.

'I told you not to go into the woods. Do you know how dangerous that was?'

'Greta went away in the woods, that's why I was finding her in the woods,' I said.

Mum didn't say anything for some time. Then she said, 'Matt, when I said Greta was still here, I meant … the happiness Greta had is here. But Greta herself is gone forever.'

Before I could say 'you're wrong,' she hugged me. I said 'ouch' because she was squishing me, but she continued. After a while she said, 'I'll have to talk with The Boss,' but I couldn't tell who she was talking to.

That night while Mum and me were eating, Dad came home. He was so early, I was surprised. He came into the living room, and stood in front of the TV so we couldn't see it. Mum put her plate on a cushion and got up. I stayed sitting on the couch.

'You're home early,' Mum said. It wasn't said like a question, but it was one of those things that actually meant a question.

'Finished early,' he said, which was an answer, but one of those ones that wasn't actually an answer. I watched his moustache twitch as he talked. I hadn't seen him for ages and ages.

It got quiet for a bit, so I said something.

'I almost finded Greta today.'

'Oh? Why were you looking for Greta?' he said.

Mum looked pale. I thought maybe there was a secret answer to the question, but I didn't know what.

'I don't know. The Boss doesn't want me to know,' I said.

'The boss? Who's 'the boss'?' he said. I thought this question was for me, but he was looking at Mum. My heart was going 'ba-dum ba-dum' like under the stethoscope.

'Oh I see,' he said, though no one had answered. 'So I'm 'The Boss', am I?'

Mum said, 'Matt, it's time for bed.'

I didn't want to sleep, I wanted to stay with Mum. But she tucked me in and went to her room with Dad. I waited five minutes, then sneaked out to listen. They were having very early night talk.

'Look, I didn't mean anything by it. I'm sorry.'

'And the fact that he ran off while you were doing your makeup?'

'I shouldn't have. I'm sorry. But maybe we need to explain what happened to Greta. If we'd explained it, this wouldn't have happened.' There was quiet.

'This happened because of you. I'm trying to protect him, and you're making a *fucking* mess.' He spoke soft, but when he said the bad word there was a smashing sound, like glass. I breathed like I was about to go underwater. Mum began speaking again.

'You want to protect him? Stop being a monster then.'

Mum's footsteps started moving until I heard her press against the door. She was so close. Soon Dad's footsteps followed.

'Monster. There. I've said it. You're the scary one. You're the one who–'

Mum stopped when a hit sound happened. I counted to ten, but then I got to ten and Mum hadn't said anything. Mum never said what happened if I got to ten. I tried to open the door, but it was locked.

'Matthew?' It was Dad, it was The Boss. I ran downstairs as the door unlocked.

Then at the bottom of the stairs, Greta was there. My mind was jumping. How was she here?

'Let's play hide and seek,' she said.

'Now? But Dad–'

'We can play until he calms down. He won't find us.'
I heard the footsteps getting closer.
'I can explain everything when we hide,' she said. We walked towards the door.
'We'll hide in the woods,' she added.
I stopped.
'Mum said the woods are bad.'
Greta shaked her head.
'No, the woods are good. In the woods you're safe. Let's go.'

We went, crouching in the black, in the trees. I heard rustling, and thought maybe it was Dad. I told Greta, and she laughed quiet.
'Don't worry,' she said, 'The Boss won't find you here. No one will.'

ROBIN EVANS

SEA LEVEL

You whittled away at the finer years of life; hours upon hours were spent
    staring into
the abyss you formed when you cut me open with a stolen surgical knife
    and a
merciless streak of curiosity. We stared, quite blankly, at the blood until we
    noticed
what it was: *the red liquid that circulates in the arteries and veins of humans*
    and
other vertebrate animals.

About a decade ago, we ambled home from school on a Wednesday. I asked
    you not
to speak to me; it was one of those bleary days where children were sent
    out in
Wellington boots and *Paddington Bear*-style raincoats because apparently
    we had to
be protected from God's torrential urination.

You never listened – not even when I tried to remind you that blood is
    nothing more
than *the red liquid that circulates in the arteries and veins of humans and*
    other
vertebrate animals – but having sanguine fluid and innards up to your
    elbows won't
help you remember what it is that you owe me an apology for.

"I can't do it. I can't stem the flow," you sob, wiping your eyes on your sleeve.
    I see
the abhorrent mixture of blood and makeup smeared over your cheekbones;
    I flinch.

At least I am above sea level – I could never choose death by drowning, for the ocean
will always appear infinite, even if I flood my lungs with salt water.

ME ME

I thought you'd be relieved but I didn't think I'd be. I saw and mother and
    daughter sing their way to
school this morning and it made me laugh.

Mornings are hard. I feel a bit small in my cold bed and the damp seems
    to be closer to me than
before but I see the sun in the mornings now and I eat breakfast. I hate it,
    but I eat it.

Evenings can be harder. I go to bed with my head spinning and my eyes
    blurry. I stay up later so
when I'm left alone with just a mind full of memories, I can pretend they
    aren't mine.

I've been very self-aware. I keep checking in with myself, "this is where
    I'm at" or "I'm feeling". They
change every hour but I had a good day yesterday, I can have a good day
    today.

People are nice. I'd forgotten who people were. You kind of skim people
    when you have someone,
like a paragraph you're not interested in. They're often the best.

So you're gone and I'm going to go play my guitar, eat fish, go to bed early
    and sing all morning long,
because me me is whole lot different from me you.

ANNA GOLDREICH

THE BODY

I THINK THERE IS A SOMETHING IN THE BELLY OF ME. I think there is
a something inside of me, I think. And I don't think because I know
because I went to the doctors and they told me and they said all these
things and they said it is my choice and then they gave me the first pill. It
had to happen this way because I am my own creature and I am not going
to be something else's. I will not be its. It will not be. I can feel all the
stones inside me, where this nearly-something creature is living. I can feel
the stones and they are pulling me down, they are hurting and they are
sinking me into myself.

You call me on the phone and you say did you get the first pill? And I
say yes and you say do you want me to come over? And I say yes. You say
we can watch a movie or something. I say yes. You say, have you told him?
I say no.

You run me a bath and you say bubbles and I say yes please and thanks
for coming over as I take off my clothes. I take off my dressing gown and
my top and my knickers but I do not take off my bra because I did not
wear a bra today and then I sit in the bath and you sit with crossed legs
on the toilet seat. You say how are you feeling and I say shit. You nod and
you laugh and you say I could've pulled it out of you, I could've got a coat
hanger and fished it out and you laugh, and I push my fingers up inside
myself like maybe I am trying to find it. I can't. My skin pimples from all
the cold of no heating and my eyes ache from all the tired of no sleep so I
shut them and go under the water. This is what it is, I am this bath and it
is me and it is growing in this bath of me and this actual bath is a womb
and I am a baby, I am a baby, I am a baby. You ask me how big is it, what is
it right now? The doctors said it is about the size of half a lime or a really

big big toe and it has sort of arms and sort of legs. You say, that's creepy, I say I know, you ask me what will happen tomorrow and I say I will take another pill and then I will miscarry. You nod.

I stand up and you pass me a towel and say you are going to make us a tea. I dry my body and I think yes, here is a body. And I think of how I like the way it goes. I like the bones in my hands, the way they want to break out of the skin. I think that perhaps they are hollow, hollow like the bones of a bird. I like this skin. I like the way it smells of salt and of the day, now it smells of soap but sometimes it smells of leaves. It is a skin that is tired and it does not need more. It is a blue of a white and I can see all the little rivers where the blood runs through and holds all the little pieces of oxygen and aliveness and it is my blood and my oxygen and my aliveness and I will not share it. I can see all the holes where the hair creeps through. All the little hairs on the body of me. Some are different and some are long and sometimes people stare at the hairs on my legs and on my armpits but I like it there because it is mine. I like the hair on my arms because they look like spider silk. Look at how the droplets from the bath cling to the hair like it is dew on the grass on the earth of me. I like all the white webs of growing on my body. Once they where red and I asked my mother will they ever go and she said yes but they never did. Now they are here and they are quietly silver and white and the skin of a fish perhaps. I like them because they say that I was once small and now I am not. I do not need more growing. I do not want to be bigger and I do not want my body to be something else's. I like it how it is and I will not share it.

I put on another top and some clean knickers and I turn off the light and we get into bed and you put your arms around me and say it'll be ok. You say, you should have washed your hair, you say, it smells like sweat. I say I know, I know but I like my smells, they make me feel better. You ask me what my mother thinks and I tell you that I have not told her because she would just get worried. You ask if I am ever going to tell him and I say no, no I don't think so, I don't want him to think he has that power. You say what, but I don't know. I shut my eyes and tell you that I do not feel guilty about it and I think maybe I should but I really don't. I tell you that I feel angry that there is a parasite inside of me and I feel like it is trying to live off my body and I am so angry because why because why because why. Because why should my body be for anyone but me? It is mine and I will not let anything twist it or contort it. I will not let this thing balloon me and I will not let it take from me. It is my body it is mine. I want to be a small thing. I want to disappear into the air. You say go to sleep because tomorrow will be a shitty day and you need to stop thinking. You kiss my head and I can feel the cry in my eyes because I hurt inside.

*

I come home from the doctors and you are still in my bed. You say, you should have woken me up, I would have come with, I tried phoning you. I say I wanted to go by myself. I say, the doctors said it would start working in a few hours. You nod and say how do you feel. I do not know. I say, they said it would hurt, I think I might be scared of how much it will hurt. I lie on the floor, you lie on the floor and I take off my shoes and socks and now we both have naked feet. I say, now we both have naked feet. We press the bottoms of our feet together and I have bigger feet than you do and we move our legs around. You say let's watch something, let's watch a documentary about other people. So we watch a documentary about asexuality. You say, if you were asexual, you wouldn't have these problems and you laugh. And then we watch a documentary about the secret life of cats, and I say I miss my cats and you make cat purr and meow noises at me, and you rub your head against mine.

I feel a bit sick. I wonder whether it is my mind or my body that is doing this. I think my insides are moving. I think they are moving and I think and I think and– yes, here is something, here is a claw from the inside of me. I can feel all the parts of me retching and moving and it is starting. It is starting and I stand and I walk to the bathroom and I sit on the loo and yes and here in my knickers is something red. And it smells of what it is. I sit on the loo and I bite my lip and I look at my knickers and they are only a bit of stained and I take them off and I look and I smell more to know it better, to distract myself. It smells of period, it smells of bloody knees and 1ps and also a bit of salt and a bit of something and another thing as well but I don't know what. You are on the other side of the door and you say are you ok, do you need anything and no, no it's fine. My belly is a hurt thing, it hurts, it hurts it hurts and I think my insides are coming out, I think I'm burning on the inside. My body does a twist and a crumple on the inside and I feel it burning. It feels bad, it feels hurt and my skin is shrinking and my skin is too little for my insides and it has things under it. I can feel them moving, I can feel them moving in my skin but there is no room they are eating me. Here, in the toilet and I do not know and I say I'm bleeding, I'm bleeding in the toilet. And my insides are sea urchining in me and I feel all the lickety wet cry sitting in my eyes trying to dripple out onto my cheeks and it is so much me and so much hurt and and I am crunching and my insides, my insides are attacking me, they are hurting me they are.

*

79

It has mostly happened but I stay on the loo for a while, and you bring me water and ibuprofen while I bleed and bleed and bleed in drips and you give me a piece of toast and you kiss my cheek and you ask me if I want another bath and you run it for me. I cannot decide whether to look in the toilet or just flush. You say you want to see it, you want to see what it looks like. I wipe and stand up and I hold the blood and pee tissue and then we look. It is a lump of something and blood and it is disgusting and maybe I want to be sick because that just came out of my insides. You say, that's disgusting, I say, I know and I throw the tissue in and flush the loo.

I take off my top and climb into the bath. There are no bubbles this time. I look at how I turn the water red from all the blood that is still coming out of me. I like it. It looks like I have tried to kill myself. You say nothing, you just watch as the water gets more and more red and maybe it will turn my skin red. I think it is strange that I can lose this much blood and be okay. If I was bleeding this much from anywhere else I might be dead and this is this is this is the wonder of my body.

REBECCA GRAHAM

FLIES

THE SOFA WAS THROWN ON LIKE A SACRIFICE. For a moment, it sat astride the burning mound of wood, cardboard, polystyrene and ash and looked almost proud. Then the fire caught and the sofa went up in flames to cheers and whistles and a dozen sets of squinting eyes. They watched it burn for a time and then began looking for something else to offer up; keen for more heat, more fire, more echoes of anarchy. Someone picked up Taylor's straw cowboy hat. She snatched it back with shrill indignation and the boys laughed.

Eddy watched all of this from the tailgate of his truck a few yards away, a beer resting loosely in his hand. From where he sat the people around the fire were no more than silhouettes and it was hard to distinguish between those he knew and those he didn't. By day, some were friends and some were not but tonight all were faceless anatomies, dark against the glare of the furnace. The weight of the tailgate shifted slightly to his left and, turning his head, Eddy saw that Grayson had sat down beside him. His features were lit soft and warm by the light of the fire. They sat silently, a space of a few inches between their shoulders, and watched as the beer-heavy figures stumbled and were mimicked by the engorged mosquitos, thankful for the dulling effect of alcohol on the human senses. The bugs dived for skin even faster than hands dived into cooler-boxes, fishing for cans.

Eddy reached for his own cooler and pulled out an Alexander Keith's. He twisted the cap off using the hem of his shirt. All the other boys did it with their bare hands and he knew that, had he been in the midst of the fireside group, he would have been mocked for his softness. But he was with Grayson and Grayson had a gentleness about him that none of the others had; he did not pretend to be callous.

Someone had pulled a mattress out from nowhere and it was being mounted on top of the pile by four boys, Jacob at the centre. They wore trucker caps and their torsos were bare – doing like their daddies had done.

'Do you ever think about the stuff that happens out here?' It was Grayson who spoke.

Eddy guided a burp into his mouth and then breathed it out in a stream through his lips.

'What kinda stuff?'

'Any kind of stuff.'

'What d'you mean?'

Grayson shrugged and looked sideways at Eddy, his dark eyes reflecting the flames. 'I don't know. Anything.' A gentle smirk played on his mouth and Eddy couldn't tell if he was being entirely serious. 'I mean, think about how far this place is from anywhere. Christ, it's just a giant sandpit in the middle of the wild. You could do anything out here and nobody would need to know.' Grayson paused to take a sip from his beer and the red maple leaf on the can rippled in the light thrown out from the fire. 'I guess I just wonder at the crazy shit that has happened out here. This place just seems to make people forget themselves.'

They both looked back to the group. A group of three were shot-gunning beers; others were seeing how close they could get to the flames without their skin catching. Jacob had his arms around Taylor and his hands were down the back of her shorts, pulling them south. She didn't seem to care that half her ass was on show. Eddy snorted, 'Some crazy shit.'

A mosquito flitted from out of the dark and landed on Eddy's arm. Before it had fed its straw through his skin, Grayson reached up and brushed it gently off. The others would have used it as an opportunity to slap Eddy as hard as they could. *Hold still*, they would say, before bringing their wide, calloused palms down on Eddy's bare skin, leaving it red and sore. *Saved your ass there.* But Grayson merely brushed his hand once down Eddy's arm, leaving no print but the upstanding hairs.

They looked at each other.

From across the pit, there came a loud wolf-whistle followed by guffaws and Jacob's thick voice, 'Enjoying your alone time, boys?' He stood atop a tailgate with his shoulders wide and his chest high as the laughter around him pumped ego through his frame.

Eddy felt his ears grow hot. He coughed and moved away slightly from Grayson. Grayson said nothing; he only took another sip of his beer whilst looking straight ahead, ignoring Jacob and the others, the boys imitating men, who were now high as kites and running out of things to burn.

*

Later that night, Jacob got Stacey onto the backseat of his truck. Soon it started to dip back and forth lightly. While the girls idly kicked at the pyre, four of the boys snuck up to the side of truck and Eddy followed. There, they crouched, listening.

At first it was just Jacob grunting rhythmically with every dip of the car. None of the boys squatting on the sand with their calves screaming wanted to listen to that, and so they began signalling to each other to creep away. Then Stacey moaned and they all froze.

'Now that's what we came for,' someone whispered and there was hushed sniggering.

They all settled back down – holding their drinks conveniently in front of their crotches – and listened intently as the couple grew louder.

Across the pit, leaning against the side of his truck, one hand deep in his pocket and the other holding up a beer, stood Grayson. The fire almost made him a silhouette like the others had been, but Eddy could just make out that his dark eyes were pointed at him. Or maybe he could just sense it. Without taking his eyes away from him, Grayson slowly raised the bottle to his lips and drank. Eddy felt he could hear the frothy liquid slip down Grayson's throat.

Jacob and Stacey grew louder still and the truck began to rock with more vigour.

Grayson raised his beer up above his head and it seemed to be a congratulatory salute as Jacob and Stacey both came loudly behind Eddy's head. The others stood up and cheered and fought for a place at the foggy window to try and get a glimpse of Stacey naked.

*

Eddy was in the forest. He had left the track and was now stumbling over roots and amongst trees that ambushed him from the dark and threatened him with his own speed. He was drunker than he had thought.

The night, in this thickness of bark and leaves, was black and full of whirring insects that either fled or pursued him. He tripped over a swollen vein in the ground and fell into a tree, jarring his shoulder. He stayed where he had fallen, clinging to the trunk, mouth gaping in shock, trying to draw in enough air.

He wanted Stacey's gasps and moans to be the reasons for his erection. He wanted the mental image of her on her back with her legs open to explain it away so that he could go back and look the others – who had all had bulges too – in the face and know that he was a man like they were men. But it was when he thought of Grayson's dark eyes and his hand on Eddy's skin that the heat rushed to his stomach.

He fumbled clumsily with the zipper of his jeans and then stopped, throwing his fist into the bark of the tree. He felt it rip his knuckles but hardly noticed any pain. 'Just drunk,' he muttered, spitting onto the ground. 'You're just drunk.'

'Eddy?' The sound seeped out of the darkness, gentle and close to where he knelt.

He let out an audible sob as a hand was placed on his shoulder so lightly that he only noticed it because of its warmth. *Just drunk.* He shuddered.

'It's alright,' Grayson murmured, his voice soothing, 'you're just drunk. You can be sick if you need to.'

They were silent for some time and the hand on Eddy's shoulder continued to pat him softly as he spat again and again into the growing pool of saliva at his knees. Eddy did feel sick but it was not the sort that came with intoxication; it was the sort that sits in the gut and festers, the sort of sickness that came with fear and shame and guilt.

Grayson moved his hand to the back of Eddy's neck, paused, and then glided up through his hair, stroking it tenderly and as if he were a child. Eddy could have slept then, with Grayson standing over him, his hand on his head. The mosquitos that landed on him drank, untouched.

And then Grayson's fingers closed around a tuft of Eddy's hair and pulled. Eddy lurched to his feet and ripped the hand away, sending up a small cloud of bugs almost too heavy to fly. The ripple of heat returned to his abdomen, calling Grayson its cause, and Eddy shook and shook and began to cry.

'Fucking fag,' he blubbed, 'dirty fucking *fag.*' He seized Grayson's hair and carried on crying and shaking and swearing until his mouth was closed by Grayson's. The launch that had meant to be an attack became a fierce embrace and the boys both stumbled in each other's grip.

Eddy felt their presence immediately. He pulled back from Grayson and looked into the faceless ring of trucker caps that surrounded them. The prolonged moment sickened his stomach with fear and told him what he had to do. He turned back to Grayson and slammed the palms of his hands into his chest, throwing him back and away.

'Dirty fucking *fag!*'

The circle closed in with Grayson at its centre, leaving Eddy on the outside – a spectator. The boys hit like they had not come from homes and soon Grayson was swallowed up and beaten down by the harder bodies.

*

Six a.m. and the sun was halfway over the belt of trees. Its blue, glassy light made the world look like it was underwater and the great belly of the pit was untouched by warmth. At its centre the black pyre sagged; there were no flames left to exalt it. Blood was brown in the dirt. Anyone would have missed it, had it not been for the flies that crawled and pulsated over the earth.

The wood was empty again and the turbulent sand in the pit was the only thing that betrayed the existence of the night before. That and the blood which was being digested and divided between a hundred black bodies.

They had left quickly when they had seen what they had done. Girls' mouths were threatened shut by boys who piled onto sweaty seats and drove away.

They ran from the pit before the morning could show them what they had already seen in the dying glory of the fire: the work of their hands. Hands that now rested on wheels and throbbed with beating organs.

They drove out of the sand in the blue morning light. Back into their lives.

JENNIFER HATHERLEY

THE GOLDEN GRAMOPHONE

THE SIGN FOR THE UNDERGROUND BURROWS INTO MY BRAIN, a little worm singing, 'Notting Hill Gate,' the words ricocheting off the back of my skull. People push past, pressing me tight against a bin. I hope that I am still visible.

'You're aware that she won't show?' my father had said on the Monday, his voice like a punctured balloon. He didn't bother to draw the air back in again and I wondered whether, with a sigh like that, there could be much of him left on the inside.

'I don't want you to go all that way, and then for her to stand you up,' he said. 'Why isn't *she* coming to see *you*, anyway?' and he looked angry in a way that I had only seen once before, when his fingers tore through the packet of Mayfair that I had wedged behind my wardrobe. He didn't look me in the eye as I explained that I was still going; instead, his gaze trailed low, resting on a crack in the floorboards, a prominent one, but apparently, irreparable.

'Don't get your mother's hopes up,' was all that he said after that.

It is a quarter past the hour, and I have run out of things to do on my phone; 'I'll be there soon,' I re-read, for the seventh time. I alternate my gaze from one side of the street to the other, scanning both of the subway entrances, willing her to appear, if only to prove him wrong.

'She may look different, you know,' my father had said on the Thursday, 'So, just be prepared for anything.' I had smirked, remembering the summer she spent a whole week walking around with a towel on her head. We didn't know what to think; all we could do was laugh. It wasn't until my father caught her at the front door one night that we understood: under the towel her golden hair was black, as black as the bottom of that ugly crevice running underneath the dining room table.

Her hair was never golden after that, only a dirty blonde colour, and everything was very different. My father didn't tell his funny stories; my younger brother started having tantrums, even though he was twelve years old; I noticed that my mother looked old. I had been staying at a friend's house on the night that she ran away. She never did wait to say goodbye.

Those July days were hot and stagnant with hating her. I thought that life would never be the same again, but when September came and school started, things went on as they always had, just without her there.

It was some months later that my chest began to hurt, just as it hurts now. It started as a dull ache. 'You have a lot of exams,' my parents told me, 'It's probably stress-related.' But when it started to drill harder, piercing my sternum, I thought, *I miss her. Yes,* I thought, *I miss her after all.*

And suddenly she is here – she is in front of me and I am struck by how beautiful she is. She wears a royal blue coat, no doubt from a charity shop. It is several sizes too big for her, the felt buttoned up from her ankles to her neck, but somehow she looks like a princess. Her hair is flaxen again, though it doesn't look quite right; the dye is a shade too light. She does not stop in her stride.

'Sorry,' she says, 'I had to walk. There was someone on the gates at the Tube station.'

She darts in front of a moving car and I follow her into the sea of people bustling back and forth through the market place. She tells me that she comes here every Saturday and that it is her favourite place; even so, she walks briskly on, rejecting the numerous stalls of cosmetics, t-shirts and mobile phone covers. She does not stop to see if I am interested in these things. I hurry after her, stealing glimpses of the exotic fabrics and snatching the scent of spices and oranges. Every so often, I catch her in profile when she turns to examine a stall, and I stare at a woman who looks almost like my sister.

She stops only once to examine a leather-bound book. I remember the piles of notebooks she left behind and I ask her if she still writes. 'Oh David and I write to each other all the time,' she says, never turning back to look at me, 'Yes, he's the one who is in love with me; the deaf albino. Just this morning I found a love poem stuck to the fridge.'

I look at her, with her laddered tights and stained t-shirt and I frown.

She sees me and she says, 'Oh, it wasn't very good, mind.'

She breaks from the main road, scooting into a side street. 'It won't be for long anyway. I'm moving in with the Hungarians next week.'

The street we have entered seems almost to be a secret passageway; none of the tourists have followed us. Hanging from the windows on either side are row after row of second-hand jackets, all for sale.

'Ivor says you're pretty by the way.'

Before I can ask who Ivor is, she is drawn to something and she is gone, her hand running over the fabric of something older and apparently more interesting than me. She has no money to pay for it though, and so we leave.

I think then that we will turn back but she darts further into the underbelly of the market. Old brick walls climb high and hold us claustrophobically close. Their rough surfaces scrape against my jacket and for a while this is all that can be heard.

When we stop she turns and says, 'I didn't know that you wouldn't be there when I left.'

I drag my fingers along the wall, exerting a pressure that crumbles the brick to dust.

'But you don't understand. I couldn't live there any longer.'

I feel the pain return between my ribs. *She* couldn't live there any longer? She is not the one who has to eat breakfast with two ghosts at the table, and a brother upstairs who has learnt what a great reaction threatening to kill himself gets. She is not the one who had to comfort their mother for the last six months, her eyes as grey as the hair on her head. She is not the one who has to beg to know where the ibuprofen is hidden every time she has a headache.

She pushes a door that I hadn't noticed was there.

'This is why I wanted us to meet here,' she says, 'I wanted to show you, so that maybe you might understand. It's the gramophone. It's beautiful.'

We stand over the golden gramophone. A ray of sunlight glimmers across the strong curve of its back.

'Isn't it wonderful?' she says, and she smiles for the first time that day. 'I can't afford it though, but one day.'

I cannot remember having seen her look this happy. I think about buying her the gramophone sometime in the future but then I realise that that would make it ours. So instead I say nothing, we stare a little while and then we leave.

We emerge outside a Tesco Metro. After we have chosen our sandwiches, she spends three or four minutes feeding loose change into the self-service machines. I am embarrassed because she holds up the queue, but she doesn't care.

After she has eaten her sandwich, she sits looking up at the skyline. 'Look at the architecture of these buildings,' she says. 'I spend days walking around the South Bank just staring up.'

The building above us is unimpressive. The ground floor is an Oxfam store, bright green and out of place against the cold stonework of

Victorian London. I follow her eye across the intricate brickwork of the upper floors, hidden from the shoppers below, but not from my sister.

'Ivor likes architecture too. I want to take him to Hampton Court.'

Hampton Court is all cobbled stone and velvet wallpaper, haunted corridors and four-poster beds. I think about how much she would like it there.

'Ivor is thirty-four,' she says casually. 'And he's gorgeous.' She produces a blurry image of the two of them, and I can only just distinguish his face from hers, but I agree nonetheless.

'Ivor knows too much about me. He knows it all. More than anyone.'

She turns inwards as she opens her crisp packet. 'Are you a virgin?' she asks, quite simply, and quite seriously. I pause a moment, trying to anticipate the direction this will take, but she interrupts before I have decided my answer. 'Because I am. I have been careful to hold onto that. I mean, Ivor thinks I'm a whore. They all do. And I let them. Hey, I told David that I'm fifteen!'

But seventeen is too close to fifteen for me to laugh.

I leave it a while before looking at my watch and telling her I need to get home.

'I will take you,' she says, and somehow, for all the twists and turns of Portobello Road, it is a ten-minute walk to our starting point.

She stands in the entrance to the subway and says, 'I know that you're angry.' And even though I need more, this is all she says. I am wondering if I should hug her goodbye when she says, 'It was nice to see you. I'm glad we got to see each other.'

She is gone before I can tell her that I'm not angry, not really. I am glad that she is happy.

On the platform it takes less than a minute for my father to call me and ask how she looked. 'Was she clean? Did she have a coat? Did she tell you her address?'

I wash over these questions and then say, 'She asked about you and Mum and Peter.'

Immediately he calls me on it, 'She didn't ask about us, did she?'

I feel my sternum start to burn. I feebly reassert my lie and tell him that my Tube is coming, 'Yes, I'm sorry. I really have to go.'

As I lean against the station wall, I notice the beauty of this underground world, hidden below the metropolis. I wait, and as I do, my phone buzzes. It's her. The text reads, 'I love you.'

It surprises me, how happy I am, and I reply, 'I love you too,' and I look up, half expecting her to be there, ready to come home with me. 'Will I see you at Christmas?' I add, and suddenly everything is snowball fights and burnt turkey and fighting over door number twenty-four on the advent calendar. I remember the snow hats we made for each other and how they were brilliant, even though we had colds for weeks after. Those family Christmases are gone now, I know, but I think about *my* London and all the places I could show her: the Frost Fair along South Bank; ice-skating at Covent Garden; every street ablaze with Christmas lights, no two the same.

A rush of warm air surges through the station and I look up from my phone. The two doors clatter apart and I join the crowd of commuters making their way home.

JOANNA HOLLINS

ALL DAY IN TOWN

All day in town and not a drop of rain.
Mother called at three. Night comes early now
winter draws in: the air cracks icily
but as yet stays dry. Trees outside look tired;
yesterday the wind came nor'westerly
sharp, bearing south by south east, a cold front
off the Atlantic. Took umbrella out.
In driving lesson master wet weather
driving and turning on wipers without
indicating by accident. Later
made proper leaf tea. Assam. Must buy milk.
Whilst doing dishes the rain starts. Alone
so lit candles, drunk tea in semi-dark.
All peaceful. Woke to the quiet pad of falling rain.

TAKE

Take two of them
give them
to me.

Larger than fire
like old perfume never
used.

Lingering in Monday,
hearing rain, hearing
heaviness.

Give me two of them,
take their skinny arms, wanting
all.

SARAH A. JONES

THE CLIFF, THE PHOTOGRAPH

The Cliff

The sea roars at the base of the cliff in a primal challenge, daring the bird to take its first flight on the salt-stiff wind. The bird ruffles its feathers, flexes its wings and, without further hesitation, launches into the air. It flaps almost comically, and then plummets towards the heaving expanse of water below.

Stupid ostrich.

Photograph

I see you like the room. My daughter calls it 'washed out' but I can tell you think it's 'lived in'. I prefer that term as well. It's a living room after all. See that patch by the doorway? Gone like that because it's been walked on so much. No, don't take off your shoes. A carpet's made to be walked on, that's my point, same thing with the rings on the coffee table and the messy books – it's *living*, see? Those bookshelves are never tidy, I read so much these days. The reason my daughter hates it in here is because the curtains are never closed, see, everything is a little faded by the sun. Look now, here it is, passing through the glass to warm up these old bones. The curtains are looking a bit pitiful, though, aren't they? All slumped into the corners of the room like that, still tied back from the time I wrestled them apart. They used to be red but with the sun – well, you can see for yourself. I bet if you were to peel the folds apart you'd see the original colours, like petals in-between bible pages, all preserved and delicate. But I'll ask you not to move them.

The cabinet? Ah, that was my wife's. It used to be in the study but after she died – oh don't be sorry, she hated it when people apologised too much. But after she died I moved it in here. There's not a lot of space so I have just put it in front of the fireplace – well technically Keith put it in front of the fire place. I doubt you know him – lives upstairs – so yes that's why it sticks out so much. Not worth a lot, but she loved it. Found it years back, at a car boot sale. It was the only thing that cut a proper silhouette on the grass that day. As soon as she saw it she crouched down in the dirt to get a look at the shelves, trying to work out whether she could save it, get a new panel for the back without ruining these carved bits on the side. I thought the whole thing was going to topple forwards and break her in half.

But then she said, 'I could do it.' She said to me, 'All it would take is a bit of work.'

Of course, the flat was full of half-finished projects of hers. Oh, I had to clear it later to make way for all the medical stuff, but back then the air was sour with paint stripper. They all just needed a bit of wood or a tool she hadn't got around to buying.

So all I said was, 'What, are you going to cut down a tree?'

'Don't be boring,' she said, 'Imagine what the wood looks like under all this paint.'

We had to tie the bloody thing to the roof of the Mini to get it home – not one of these modern Minis, mind – from the sky it probably looked like there was a cabinet floating down the A47.

It locks, I have the key on a string in the kitchen and – I'll tell you a secret. Inside that cabinet isn't gold or anything else. No, I lock away *Coronation Street*. Only thing in there is a television set, nothing else. I watch it in the evenings, you know, when I'm too tired to read. Old eyes, see. But I shut it away if I have guests, like yourself, or if I am missing Meredith. Hated televisions, she did. I like to think that somewhere she scowls at me when I watch it. Some days I swear she's about to storm out of the kitchen and tell me to turn the bloody thing off.

I must say, when you came up to me in the park I was a bit shocked. Nobody talks in the park, let alone asks for a photo. I'm sorry if I seemed a bit out of sorts. People don't talk to old men. Usually they just stare at the owl for a bit and wander off. My poor dog gets so jealous. But you looked so familiar. I didn't want to say anything at the time, but have we met before? Are you from around here? No? Have you been on the television or something?

Yes, sorry. Where do you want me to sit? The sofa? I'll call the animals in. Both strays, you know. The dog I found about a year back, in the garage in the middle of the night. God knows how it ended up there. A weird noise had woken me up and I'd rolled over and asked Meredith if she needed anything, and as I woke up a bit more, arm stretched out into the empty side of the bed, I heard the noise again. Grabbed a torch and traced it to the garage and found this fellow crouching under the Mini, all dusty and frightened. I lured him in with some food and he spent the night at the foot of our bed, that small meaty snore of his going like bellows. The next day I rang the police – to see if he was missing, you know, but the officer told me he wasn't. So, that afternoon, I went out and bought him a collar. Needn't have done – he never wanders far. But I liked the way he looked, way he belonged.

The owl, pretentious thing, isn't nearly as interesting. Don't look so surprised. She just sort of showed up one day at the window – not long after Meredith went – and demanded attention. Got the RSPB round in a flash, I can tell you. The woman upstairs, who lived there before Keith, was on the phone right away all worried for her hamster – refused to open the window in case it managed to get in. Silly old biddy. An owl's not going to go for a pensioner, and as long as the hamster stayed in the cage it would've been fine. All it would have done is sat and watched her. Maybe that's what she was scared of. Well, as it turns out, the bird's a pretty rare breed, worth quite a bit, apparently. They tried to take her to a sanctuary but she got so flustered that they left her with me – they were all concerned she'd do herself some harm. Got huge dark eyes, hasn't she? They don't reflect anything back. Kind of like yours, actually. All clever, like there's something whirring away at the back of your head. Must have the ladies falling over you. Aha, I know that smile – I'll say no more. My, how your ears have gone pink. Alright, there's no need to crush that camera case of yours. Shall we get this done, then? I'll see if I can get the bird to stay put on my shoulder so she can be in the shot.

There.

Did it work? I didn't see it flash. Can I see? God, I look even worse than the curtains. I swear in my head I'm still twenty-five.

Oi! Sorry, excuse the dog. He gets a little unsettled sometimes. Doesn't happen a lot these days but if something spooks him it takes him a few moments to calm down. It must have been the camera which set him off. I'll put him in the kitchen. Are you sure you don't want a hot drink? I only have tea, I'm afraid. Meredith was the big coffee drinker; the place always used to stink of it. I didn't really mind but it used to circulate the rooms. You could taste it on the dust. Well, at least it covered the smell of paint stripper. One moment.

There.

Are you quite alright? Hovering at the door like that? I heard some rattling. No, I haven't locked you in. You just turn them both – just move back a moment – like this, see? No need to act so twitchy. Come and look at this a moment, I just grabbed it from the kitchen. It's a newspaper from a few weeks back. Crisp, isn't it? I ironed out the creases. That's the trick to keeping them, you know? Well, my daughter's pretty famous in her own way, you see, and she always sends me a copy of every paper she makes it into. I don't read the papers myself, too depressing. Meredith used to call them 'Ghost Stories', but I make sure to keep these safe. She's got her mother's gift for drawing, lucky thing, and she's always loved drawing faces. When she was a teenager she used to wander round the streets with a camera, looking for profiles to capture and draw. Kind of like you, eh? She's only gotten better, now, though. One moment, let me find it.

What *is* the matter with that dog? I'm sorry, he's not done this for years. And – don't jump up like that, here, come sit – it's just the phone. No matter, just ignore it. Here it is. I love the look on people's faces when I show them these pictures. She's so talented, they almost look like photographs. All she gets given is a short description from the police, you know. Just something like: six foot two, handsome, big brown eyes, camera. And the next day she'll be given a different one. These con men. They're always changing – they're chameleons. And it's my daughter's job to strip back all the layers. You know, she's like her mother, always getting behind the surface of things. She finds what's underneath. But look. Tell me. Doesn't this one look ever so much like you?

NATHANIEL KING

PILLOWS IN A CEMETERY

waking up once more in canada
sunshine like a vascular chute
torn autumnal thighs
i am a breath of wind
touching your neck
how casually you fit
in my arms with cheeks of fur
i am turning into a fir tree
nice to meet you.
how very strange of you
to disappear in wool coat
down an enclave across a grave
my sweet *chemise*
i still touch you like
a bag full of leaves.
i am an intravenous drop
on the surface of a snowman
melting softly and
wondering why no-one ever
put pillows in a cemetery
how do those skeletons sleep
softly whispering
like the first murmurs
from an espresso pot.
wondering who ever
imagined an outburst
so hopeless,
the ceiling fan splinters
and flays
my last bouquet.

how white your body
at this moment, glazing
over with the weight of all windows–

preternaturally clear. you are
a sleeping cog in a windmill, a
swiss watch in my arms.

OCCUPATIONAL HAZARDS

they put me to work in the typing pool
i was howling into a six-inch dictaphone
all the names i had never experienced
all the faces who wouldn't give me pay
they told me to keep going under the obsolescence
first time i stayed it had been
scripted and carefully arranged
the terms of my contract were up i was
returned to the sweet bosom of no-one
feeling pretty civilian and without cause
i wondered the tundra for days
visiting the electric cemetery
i rubbed out all my circas
asked the mortician to reserve
a bed on the third night of ramadan.
two days before bankruptcy

they changed the locks and left a
note in cellophane saying
we don't have the mind
or hands to choke you

so wait bashful
for yr body to sub-zero,
it only takes two days.

LUKAS KOUNOUPIS

DON'T GAZE TOO LONG

RONALD'S EYES TRACKED THE MASS OF DAMP spreading through the ceiling. The hanging lamp swayed to the war's rhythm. Dull, repetitive, irritating. It didn't work. And no one cared enough to fix it. He'd got used to it by now, in a way. The lazy squeak, while the radio on the shelf chirped some sort of folk music. Outside, the Vietnamese peddlers' cries were giving way to the whistling and wooing of prostitutes. It was almost comforting.

Another glass came crashing down onto the counter, which was already strewn with them; some standing, most toppled: the remains of the platoon's annual memorial party. A day dedicated to those who'd fallen in battle, always unsurprisingly devolving into a game of who can get hammered first. Speed was a crucial factor.

He sat next to Aaron, who wasn't taking part in the contest. Aaron had just deprived a private of his drink, causing a series of grunts as a response, with the occasional banging. With every thump the glasses rattled in complaint.

Ronald sighed. Sweat trickled down his face, leaving behind that unbearable itch. A crappy little fan sitting on the bar was all they had. Forget the Cong. The heat was what he hated most about this place.

Aaron threw him a hasty glance, then his head sank. "Sorry, Sergeant." He took hold of his glass. "Come on guys, let's give them a real one."

"Fallen, but never forgotten."

He put it down.

Ronald took a sip of his lukewarm beer. He sat with his back against the counter, watching the specks of sunlight that still seeped through the blinds.

Most of the men had left. They'd had their drinks, and the few that were sober enough afterwards paid their respects too.

"Brothers in Arms" the higher-ups loved calling them. Just a collection of gauzy shapes and murky faces. Except for one. There was one face Ronald remembered well, probably always would. For most it was of a wife, or a daughter. Son, maybe. Something pleasant. Hell, anything. Anything other than that smile. But no, Brandon's smile was carved into Ronald's mind.

He wasn't smiling now. He'd been quiet all day, sitting on the far edge of the bar, gorging on his whiskey. Ronald signaled the bartender with a waggle of his fingertips.

He came closer, a slight tremor in his movements. Understandable. No one liked the prospect of a bunch of big, burly oafs letting loose in his establishment. And it was a fair bet that the prospect of a whole army of them letting loose in his country didn't seem much more appealing.

"Get them another round," Ronald whispered, slipping some folded đồng bills into his palm. He got a confused look. "Same as before."

"Is on the house too?" the bartender asked, loud enough for everyone to hear. Ronald rolled his eyes.

Brandon chuckled. "Feeling generous, Ronnie?"

"Only get one chance a year to do this," Ronald said.

Brandon rid his bottle of its last drops. "Courtesy of our fallen heroes." The bartender was about to pour some more into a glass, then Brandon snatched another bottle from him.

Aaron was frowning. He turned towards Ronald. "Sorry, Sergeant, but—"

"Don't need to say that all the time."

"Yeah, sorry... okay, won't happen again, Sergeant. I—"

"I meant 'Sergeant'," Ronald said. "Apologise all you want. Almost makes me think I'm in the right."

"You are," Aaron said. "Brass is wrong on this one." He looked at Brandon, "Don't care if he's getting the job done, way he's doing it still ain't right. And they just let him do whatever the hell he wants."

"Can't expect them to lock up their poster boy," Ronald said.

"Didn't know that gave him a free pass to use civilians as bait. It ain't—"

Brandon peered over at Aaron. Aaron averted his gaze. "Look, all I wanted to say is, maybe he's had enough to drink?"

"Don't worry about it."

That didn't seem to satisfy him. "Uh... okay, it's just... well, there's only so much you can do if he loses it. We're pretty much expecting you to keep him in line, you know? Better not make things any harder than they already are."

"Couldn't do that if I tried."

Aaron was about to open his mouth again, instead settling for a solemn nod.

"Might make this your new assignment, Sarge," Brandon said. "You just keep providing the booze; I'll win the actual battles."

That he did. Wins all over the board since Brandon was made lieutenant. Some murmurs about "unconventional methods" were quickly stamped out. Ronald was the annoying fly the brass just couldn't seem to swat. He'd been letting them know about every one of Brandon's little incidents, from the first, till the most recent.

Thinking of it now, the first time seemed mild compared to his later deeds. They'd been travelling through an abandoned town. Mostly abandoned. A few inhabitants were still rummaging around their homes, scavenging for anything with some sort of value. The platoon had been bogged down by a minefield. Not a rare thing. They sprinkled them where you least expected any. Cheap way to take out a few dozen chumps.

Not with Brandon around. He'd whistled at one of the townsfolk crawling through some garbage, told him there was a hidden stash of supplies in one of the buildings ahead. Having bought every single thing he was told, he started racing towards it, into the mines. Legs striding, arms flailing, his whole body seemed to drift loose. Full of hope, for a few seconds.

Wasn't full of much after those seconds. He burst open and all that hope splattered through the air, some of it oozing through the dirt in pulpy bits. By the end of that day the platoon had reached its destination; a job well done, with no casualties. None that mattered, anyway.

Ronald had tried getting to the villager, but Brandon would have none of it. He held Ronald firm to the ground, with what was probably great ease. Ronald had thought he could force his way past. He tore at Brandon, yelling, spit and all that. Had a bit of a spark in him back then; he was still fresh from eating up sermons about heroism. Brandon just stood with his back turned, outstretched arm ensuring that Ronald would not get a chance to disrupt his plan. After it was done Ronald found himself staring at Brandon for a good long while. All he received in return was a smile.

He was betting on more than that tonight. Brandon was returning some patrons' looks, and one after the other they backed down. Once they had all settled for staring either at the floor or the ceiling, Brandon treated them to a lump of spit. It landed next to a group of them. That warranted a few grumbles, but still nothing major.

"Not a fan of the slums?" Ronald asked. All he got was silence. "Want to choose a different bar next year?"

"God forbid there's fewer slopes in that one."

"Thought you'd like it. Thought you loved having... slopes around. Always find some use for them."

That got him a laugh.

"Don't you?"

That got him a stare. Aaron pulled at Ronald's sleeve, his voice trembling almost as much as his hand. "Wh-what are you—"

Brandon groaned as he got up from his stool. He wobbled towards Ronald, towering over him. As he leaned in close, the stink of alcohol in his heavy breath wafted into Ronald's nostrils. "You fishing for a confession, Ronnie?"

Brandon was smiling now. "Admission of my... what did you call them... detestable war crimes? Getting innocents killed in order to achieve my goals?" His voice dropped to a hush. "You know, even I've lost track of all my bullshit excuses. Combat conditions? Collateral damage? They always fall for that one, right?" He raised his tone again. "Poor souls, tragically caught in the crossfire."

"You really do get off on it," Ronald said.

"You telling me you don't?" He tilted his head to the right. "Not even a little?"

Ronald wasn't sure if Brandon was still toying with him, or asking a serious question. He also wasn't sure which one of the two possibilities bothered him more. And the longer Brandon didn't talk, the more Ronald thought he was waiting for an answer.

"No," Aaron said. "He's— he's not sick like you."

"Ouch, 'sick'. That's harsh." Brandon put a hand on Aaron's shoulder, who flinched back. "Are you like him? Thinking you're gonna save all of them?" He waved his arm across the room. "If they don't want to chew their own leg off, they don't get to complain that someone's doing it for them. Was never gonna be pretty, it'll leave a few scratches."

"More than a few," Ronald said.

Brandon shook his head. "You can't see past your own whining anymore. Always go running to the captains, ready to rat. You ever think about what happens if we all had the same stick up our ass? Hmm? We rot. Numbers drop, your pals the slopes here get some courage; they move back in, have their way with us." His smile was gone. "If you think what I'm doing isn't pretty, wait until you see the alternative." Brandon started walking back to his stool, then stopped halfway.

"You've gotta learn, Ronnie. You don't learn, you end up like every other miserable bastard that died over here. Just another number written off a list. If you're lucky someone shouts out your name while getting wasted in some shithole." The bottle was back in his hand. "Don't feel bad for any of these bastards giving you puppy eyes. They got themselves into this fucking mess, now they try to get rid of the only help their sorry asses were lucky enough to ever—"

"We don't want your help," a shout was heard. It was a younger man, sitting at a table.

Brandon's brow rose, followed by a giggle.

The man persisted. "You make everything worse."

Brandon made his way to the table. He stopped before the man, who got to his feet, meeting Brandon's lazy eye with quite the glare. "You come to our home, and you shoot people, you steal, and you don't respect anyone. You cannot help. You cannot do anything, and when you lose you blame us because you are useless and you cannot—"

The bottle shattering on his face cut him off. He bent to the right, flopping down on the ground. Brandon kneeled over him, flipping the man's head upwards. He flicked a glass shard from his cheek, holding it between his fingers. He then started ramming his fist into the man's face, the shard ripping its way through.

Ronald stood close, unmoving, like everyone else. Aaron was next to him, eyes darting back and forth. They settled on Ronald. "Aren't you gonna do something?" He didn't get a response. Taking a deep breath, Aaron stepped forward, ready to lunge himself at Brandon. That's when Ronald stretched out his arm, blocking his path. He guessed it was surprise that made Aaron halt for a moment. Didn't take long for that surprise to turn into anger. He started all but clawing at Ronald to get through, shouting at him. None of it worked.

Brandon was finished in less than a minute. He walked out, shouldering past people. Little remained of the man's face. Some of his limbs were twitching.

"He's done," Ronald said.

"Yeah, look at him," Aaron said. "Why didn't you—"

"Brandon. Slaughtering an unarmed civilian, unprovoked, witnesses. Dishonorable discharge, at least. If this opens up a real investigation into everything else..."

That only made Aaron run his palm over his face.

Ronald glanced over at the empty whiskey bottles. A few minutes later he walked out of the bar, while Aaron found himself staring at Ronald for a good long while.

RACCOON

my fuck-up friend with sleeves too short sits
on the chipped taupe paint wood
porch deck that in the summertime my dad sticks
a leaking hose under to drown the raccoons that live there
like i kinda want god to do with my house
i pray one day the windows & doors
never open and floodwater rises past the
basement blotting the bloodink words of my sister's journal
while my friend says she's hot and
i say, i know she is i know she is
i hope the water washes away
the condom & cigarette in my tornjean pocket
and my two fingers in
her balmy mouth, blurred & open
i think
my mouth looks like that

ANNIE

we cut ourselves open and
replaced our sulfurous citydirt blood
with cheap ice cream and cigarettes we smoked
sitting by the river that smells like
shit when it rains too much
trying to shine like the hot silver tray of perfumes
next to your winterflesh pink bed we laid on
and took our clothes off in front of open windows
because we were two girls
trying to be more than two girls
and ending up with cemetery sunburns
and soft diner food bellies
and uneven uncareful boyhand imprints
around our throats
almost as unsteady as our hands
when we tried to paint ourselves into masterpieces
two Virgin Marys
in the cold damp basement of my house
queens on a broken pullout couch jagged mattress
springs leaving holes in our back
where we wanted angel wings to go
dad yelling at me for stealing a beer from the fridge
while you brushed your hair
with the precision I used to apply red lipstick
just to get it smudged on the edge of a bottle
and when we left parties early together
we felt like god walking around Chicago downtown at 2am
the street an altar and our high heels
bridging the gap between heaven and earth
and we'd listen silent and empty as church
for the way men called at us with their cigarillo smoke signals
crying from their islands alone for us
we'd never admit it Annie
but it felt like worship

MIRANDA LANGFORD

SIGHTSEERS

THE CITY WAITS AT DUSK: ORANGE, SWOLLEN WITH THE DAY, it breathes out. Summer comes in March. Up on the hill children listen to the evening, feeling the weight of it. Over a mountain of tin roofs, bells call in the evening mass; dogs yowl, mate and yawn; water hangs in the air, close and hot but not quite touching; a brother screams at his little sister.

*

The brother rounds a corner. Running ahead, footsteps a samba, he remembers the way of the narrow, winding streets here, knows he is at the edge of something. The sister cries, salt tears mixing with the salt left on her skin by the ocean. Itchy, too warm, she doesn't want to go. She thinks of their mother back in the house, scared to walk the streets unprotected because of children just like them, children who know English swear words and only smile when they want something. Children who laugh at the sister's new plastic sandals. The shoes are too big but she will grow, and when the straps are tighter she will be able to catch up with her brother and stop him without falling down. For now, every step is a hazard.

From the top of the coloured steps, they will be able to look out over the whole city. A gap between two yellow houses will reveal the skyline, and the thousands of homes built into the mountains, each one leaning towards the coast and baring its back to Christ the Redeemer. They will see all the way down to the beach. They will point at the spot on the rocks where the brother taught the sister to do a standing dive earlier today, and they will watch as the restaurants turn their evening lights on one-by-one at the edge of the sand, waiting to see if they can hear American karaoke from all the way up here or the cheers of a televised football game. The crest will give them a vantage point so they will see the others coming up before they are seen themselves. The brother will jump out and make that boy apologise to the sister, and perhaps he will even make him kiss her shoes for good measure, so he knows the boy means it.

The sister catches up as her brother slows down. They both rest, breathing hard, and the brother smoothes his hand over the metal lump tucked into his side, checking it is still there. The coldness of it bites through his shorts pocket to the skin underneath. He doesn't know what will happen if his mother notices it is missing, but he won't let himself think about that. He will be able to return it later that day, and no one will be any wiser.

*

The children first saw the view from the car, on the drive down to the beach earlier that day. The guide had stopped for a few minutes, to allow their parents to take photographs of the sprawling buildings, of the homes made out of nothing but congregated metal and plastic sheets. Laughing, the mother said she had thought her windows needed a clean. It looked like a single gust of wind would blow everything into the ocean. At the back of the car, sitting behind locked windows, the children struggled to see it themselves, and caught their own reflections instead. As the guide released the handbrake and they began to roll back down the cobbled road, the sister noticed a burst of colour, yellow, green and blue, slapped across steps that cut into the hillside. She saw writing, a childish scrawl in thick black paint, before the wheels carried her away and out of sight.

Although she could not make out any pictures, the steps reminded the sister of her playground back home. In September her favourite teacher, the one who holds after-school art classes and organises trips to the bowling alley, convinced the school board to let the pupils paint the dull-grey wall that hems them in during playtime. The wall stretches along two sides of the playground, just low enough for the Year Sixes to look over but too high for anyone else. Each class was given a section to make their own, carefully and evenly divided.

Afterward, the sister's parents had compared the slap-dash mural to obscene graffiti. The sister had seen the bad words spray-canned on empty shop-fronts and abandoned petrol stations, however, and knew what the rude doodles on the bridge over the river meant. She had to ask her brother, but she knew what they meant. She knew the wall in her playground was different. Her wall was wonderful.

One day the sister sat in front of the wall for an entire lunch break, armed with marker pens and chalk pastels snatched from the art cupboard. Crouched down on the worn ground, laddering her pink tights and ignoring the calls from her classmates, she took five square inches for her own. Carefully and delicately she sketched a miniature house, with rainbow walls and a turret instead of a chimney. A family waved from inside the windows, a mother and father with one daughter outlined in black to make her stand out from the others, and no brother to take up space in an already too-small area. In tiny letters, the sister inked her initials in the bottom left-hand corner of the wall, small enough so no one could make them out but her.

*

As they stood on the rocks by the ocean that afternoon, the brother tried to get his sister to take her shoes off. He showed her how easy it was to grip the slimy, algae-covered surface with bare feet, bouncing up and down on the edge, but she tightened the straps even more, making red welts form around her ankles. The brother had his hands outstretched, ready to push her off out of frustration when a tall, red-faced boy came up behind them.

You go to my church, the boy said. I know your mother.

The boy looked at the sister then, and noticed her feet. The sandals looked like two giant blue starfish trying to eat her toes, and the red-faced boy laughed.

They are too big for you. They would fit my sister better.

They're new, the sister mumbled. She tried to spread her feet to make them look as large as possible, and her brother jumped over to her rock to shield the shoes from view, bringing himself closer to the intruder. Silently, he wondered what kind of Santa Theresa kid got sunburn. The red face towered over him; the brother reasoned that the boy had to be at least three classes above.

Give them to me after Mass, the boy said. But clean them before. I don't want them to smell like you and your fat mother.

*

The sister told her brother about the colourful steps while they jumped over waves. Their parents sat on the beach guarding towels and bags, clutching on to their camera and phones. Every few minutes they shouted at the children over the crashing water, urged them not to venture too far out and asked them to smile for another photo. The brother obliged every time, until the minute they put the camera down and looked the other way. Then he was free to push his sister's head under.

When she came up for air the sister slapped him across the stomach, threatening not to tell him her secret unless he stopped trying to drown her. The brother relaxed his arms and listened, but only for a few seconds. Before she'd finished her sentence, he had already formulated a plan. He was bright and manic with the promise of something new; bored already, only a few days into their holiday, the brother longed for the chance to break away and leave his whining mother and father behind. He was an adult now. He doubted the family had noticed the darker shadows under his arms and in the centre of his chest, and it'd been a while since he undressed in front of them so knew only he had seen the changes under his swimming trunks. There was a new feeling that kept rising up into his head and chest every time he was treated like a child, a feeling that made him want to scream and punch walls and dunk his little sister's head under water. He felt like the mountains behind him would crumble into the ocean if only they knew what was inside him. With the rise and fall of every new wave he ached, feeling simultaneously enormous and tiny, as if he could just as much halt the ocean with one hand as he could curl up and be carried away by it, out along the current and into the distance until he disappeared from view.

By mid-afternoon the family has returned to the guesthouse halfway down the winding streets. While their parents enjoy a lazy nap by the poolside, the children creep under the loungers and pull a camera out from their mother's bag. The brother quickly hides it in the waistband of his shorts. His sister is nervous, and can't shake the fear that they will get found out. As her brother grabs her hand and roughly pulls her behind him, carefully edging around the garden's gate without making it creak, she begins to cry. Her new shoes are already uncomfortable, and it is a long way up to the top of the hill without a guide and the soft backseat of a car.

When they are out of earshot of the guesthouse, the brother shouts at his sister, running ahead of her. The sun starts to disappear behind the blue mountains, and unless they reach the top quickly they won't be able to see the houses and the painted steps clearly enough, and will have to abandon their adventure. Catching up, the sister rounds a corner at the same time as her brother, where they come face-to-face with themselves.

The other siblings are just as surprised to see them. The brothers look at each other, wide-eyed, and then at the sisters standing just behind them. The other brother and sister are the same, except their skin isn't sunburnt and their clothes are a little more dusty; the sister sees the other even has new shoes like hers, and both their eyes are sore and red. All four children breathe heavily, and are not sure if it's just the altitude that makes the air thinner. They all think of their mothers at the same time.

One boy suddenly spits out a stream of fast, angry Portuguese, his eyes round and fearful. He thrusts his hand into the waistband of his shorts, pulling out a shining silver handgun, huge and heavy in his small hands. He brandishes it in the air, pointing it at the doubles, and motions for them to empty their pockets.

The English sister only has a packet of gum. She shakes as she hands it over to her twin, not noticing that the girl does not want to take it from her. The brother thinks about bowing his head, signing that he is just as empty-handed, but he knows they have seen the bulge in his side, the bulge that is not quite big enough to be another gun. He slowly pulls the camera out and offers it forward.

The other brother takes it without a word, stuffing it back in the waistband where the gun rested only moments before. He starts walking backwards up the hill, gun still pointed at his victims, then turns and runs, his sister falling over her shoes to keep up, the gum flying from her hand and coming back down to lie on the road.

As two figures grow smaller in the distance, the other two remain still, casting long shadows. It is as if the brother and sister have lost control of their limbs. One after the other they slump onto the cobbles feet from the painted stairs. Reaching for his sister, wanting to pull her close rather than push her down, the brother knows it is not really the gun that scared them, or the loss of their mother's camera. He hears the bells toll in the distance; they are the same clangs and calls of their church back home, only quieter, smaller, less obtrusive. He holds the little girl tight, rubbing her back reassuringly. She is crying again, not understanding what she has seen, but suddenly wishing she was back behind the window of a minivan, allowing the wheels to roll her backwards, away from rainbow-painted walls and houses that lean towards the sea.

JO LAVENDER

STACCATO

'When I'm asleep, dreaming and lulled and warm,
They come, the homeless ones, the noiseless dead.
...
Out of the gloom they gather about my bed.
They whisper to my heart; their thoughts are mine.
"Why are you here with your watches ended?
From Ypres to Frise we sought you in the Line."
In bitter safety I awake, unfriended;
And while the dawn begins with slashing rain
I think of the Battalion in the mud.
"When are you going out to them again?
Are they not still your brothers through our blood?"'[1]
S. Sassoon.

A nd now you want to go back to those brothers. Rivers sighed and
uncapped his pen. He drew a sheet of paper towards him, and wrote:
'Craiglockhart Psychiatric Hospital.
Edinburgh, Scotland.
Medical Assessment, 8th Nov., 1918.
Assessor: Captain W. H. R. Rivers.
Patient: Captain S. Sassoon.
Diagnosis: Shellshock.
Verdict:
Rivers listened to his watch measure out a few seconds, curling and
uncurling his fingers and watching the light play along the tube of the pen.

'Well?' Sassoon asked, voice brusque. Rivers twirled the pen. He looked at the word *Verdict* again, and then up at Sassoon. His friend. His patient. The poet. *Can I do this? Can I send him back? Make him one of the 'citizens of death's grey land, drawing no dividend from time's to-morrows?'[2] Will he go back and die?*

Sassoon twitched and started to thrum his fingers on the desk. 'Don't just *look* at me, Captain, please,' he said. 'I need an answer.'

Rivers rubbed his eyes, pushing the poem away. 'I'm trying to decide. I have a duty to get you back to the Front, but I *also* need to make sure you're fit.'

Sassoon turned away. Rivers went to open the window, looking down at the gravel, which lay in the sun four floors below. He was aware of Sassoon's heavy breathing in the silence, overlaid by a woodpecker rapping at a tree. He hated this moment: the moment after the tri-monthly boards, when the patients to be cleared came to him, and he wrote their future.

'*Now the soldiers he smiled at are most of 'em dead,*'[3] he thought bitterly, and tried to turn his attention back to Sassoon.

'You still have symptoms of shellshock, Siegfried,' he said, careful to keep his voice gentle. 'You aren't really fit to go back.'

'Going back is the only thing I can do.' Sassoon began to tug at the thread on the breast of his jacket. His file said he'd thrown his Military Cross in the Thames. *But how*, Rivers wondered, *can you be ashamed of a medal awarded for lives saved? Hours under gunfire, bringing in the dead and wounded, and you threw away the medal.*

'You have nothing to feel guilty for,' he said. 'Being safe isn't a crime, and you fought hard.'

'I don't care. Not about the fighting. Or the honour. Or the war.' Sassoon tugged more frantically on the thread. Taut, relaxed. Taut, relaxed. Rivers felt as though Sassoon was twisting up his frustration and fear and releasing it with a jolt.

'I just want to go back to my men.'

'Do you think returning will protect them?' *It won't. You can't do anything.*

'No.' Sassoon's mouth contorted. 'That's up to our fine generals, isn't it?' He sat back, resting a hand over his face.

Rivers poured the tea, which was now lukewarm. He and Sassoon had been having tea together at 13:00 every Monday for nine months. The gesture held the comfort of familiarity, and the awareness of an imminent goodbye. 'Here.'

Sassoon took the cup. He added sugar and stirred once clockwise, twice counter-clockwise, as he always did, then struck the spoon three times against the rim of the cup.

I've done my duty. He wants to go back. Shellshock or not. He wants to go. But duty doesn't mix kindly with friendship.

Sassoon met his eyes, and Rivers looked away. The pen attracted his gaze, smooth and lean in the strip lights.

'Captain Rivers... the taxi is due at 14:00...'

Rivers took up the pen and weighed it in his hand, then set it to the paper. He could hear blood drumming in his ears as he stared at the white stretch below the nib. *Thud-thud. Thud-thud.*

Looking up, he found Sassoon also watching the nib. When Rivers didn't write anything, Sassoon raised his eyes. He could almost hear Sassoon's thoughts – *Clear me. I'm fit.* He picked up his tea again, and Sassoon exhaled angrily.

'Do you really think I'm unwell?'

'I... am not entirely sure, Siegfried.' *At least, I'm not sure what to do.*

'What are we coming to, if the doctor doesn't know?'

'Doctors never know as much as they like to pretend.'

'I've been here for nine months. Golf. Afternoon tea. Regular meals and clean sheets. I can't stand it anymore.'

No, of course you can't. 'When I'm asleep, dreaming and lulled and warm, They come, the homeless ones, the noiseless dead.'[4] *They won't leave you to rest.* 'Love drove me to rebel. Love drives me back to grope with them through hell.'[5] Rivers pinched the bridge of his nose hard, trying to get Sassoon's words out of his head.

'You knew it would happen. You knew I couldn't stand sleeping safe at night with my men being slaughtered like cattle.'

The hint of accusation in Sassoon's voice made him blanch. His friend looked tired, his hand still twitching on the thread of his uniform. He was baby-faced, clean-shaven, pale in khaki. Sassoon was thirty-one, but nights of trenches and guns and poetry seemed to have frozen him. More than any patient Rivers could remember, Sassoon looked young. But his eyes were dark and starless.

Sassoon placed his cup on the desk and plucked the thread harder.

Rivers watched. 'You aren't better, Siegfried.' He forced decision into his tone and took up the pen.

Sassoon leaned across the desk and grabbed his hand, so abruptly that a line of ink dashed across the form. Sassoon's eyes fixed themselves on his, months of the trenches swallowed in their depths.

'What difference does it make when facing the guns? I want to go back.'

Rivers could feel sweat between their hands, and he didn't know whose sweat it was. Sassoon's pulse beat against his skin. *Like gunfire.* Then Sassoon released him and sat back.

Rivers felt his face twist. He set his pen to the line; his hand moved instinctively, and a moment later, he was looking at stark black strokes. Clumsy and half-detached. 'Cleared for duty.' *The full stop seemed to step away from the words, inky with guilt.*

'There.' *I've done it.*

He watched him stand and salute.

'See me again, Sassoon.' Rivers looked up at him. 'When the war is over.'

'I would like that, sir.' Sassoon smiled thinly.

When the war is over. If it's ever over. 'In fifty years, when peace outshines ... They'll envy us the dazzling times, When sacrifice absolved our earth.'[6]

'Goodbye, Captain Rivers.'

He's going back to die. Mad Jack, they call him in the trenches. Mad Jack, going back to die.

The door closed behind Sassoon, and the office grew quiet.

Rivers rubbed his face and looked at the paper again. It was his writing at the top, with the scratch of accidental ink next to his statement: *'Cleared for duty.'*

I cleared Siegfried Sassoon for duty.

Cured, cleared, clean. Mad Jack, clean of shellshock. Rivers bent his head and pressed the pads of his thumbs to his eyes, envisioning the taxi outside. He was too high up to hear its engine, but nonetheless its chug was loud in his ears. He pressed until his eyes hurt, blinked, and placed his palms on the desk so he could feel his blood pulsate. *Thud-thud. Against the hard cuffs of his uniform, his hands looked fragile.* Khaki makes flesh translucent.

Cured, cleared, clean. Cleared to go back. Back where he could walk the tiptoe-top of the trench at night and drop down into the grass beyond, whistling to the guns until their fire found him. *He's better. Fit.* Rivers got to his feet and walked around the desk, looking at Sassoon's file upside-down.

Cured, cleared, clean. *I cured him. I put on a doctor's face. I sat in silence when he needed silence, and then I goaded him into guilt. I cured him to go back to the Front and die.*

He dipped the end of his pen into the now cold tea and watched the drops splash back, tracing the surface with ripples. A series of sharp taps broke the silence. 'Captain Rivers?'

'Come in.'

The Sergeant entered. 'I've come for the files.'

'I cleared six.'

The man had a scrubby face, like pebbledash. 'Thank you, Captain. They'll be singing your praises at HQ, sir.'

Rivers smiled, leaning against the desk. 'Oh, I doubt it, Sergeant. I cause too much trouble for that. Too many requests for supplies they can't spare. Just a moment.'

He found the papers and handed them over. *Andrews, Arkley, Colson. Hardy, Jones, Sassoon.*

'Thank you, Sir.' The Sergeant saluted and left.

It was a relief to hear the door close. He looked at the paperwork waiting to be sorted. He had promised to find Anderson a new room on the south side of the building; his nightmares were worse when he could hear rain in the trees. Hollins had requested spare blankets. He had lain in No-Man's-Land for sixty-three hours, and the chill of it followed him like a ghost. Rivers hoped he could find another blanket. The board said they didn't need more. *No,* he thought. *Does a man who laid so long in the cold, breathing with the dead and watching his own blood drain* need *another blanket?*

He should visit Hollins. It was cold. *I'll buy him warm socks, the next time I can get into town.*

He swept a hand in front of his eyes and went to the window. The gravel lay empty in the sunlight. The taxi was gone. Rivers had wanted to accompany Sassoon to London, but Sassoon had refused. He'd be fine, he'd said. Just fine. The Army would look after him.

Rivers stared at the trees outside, disturbed by how peaceful it was. Even the woodpecker's rattle had stopped, as if it had followed Sassoon. *'To the land where all Is ruin, and nothing blossoms but the sky.'*[7]

Another knock. There was no peace at Craiglockhart. One of the kitchen girls came in, rattling fresh tea, collecting the old tray.

'The new patient should be here in five minutes, Captain Rivers.'

'Thank you.'

'You're welcome, sir.'

He smiled wryly. The patient wasn't new at all, but a relapse case – Rivers remembered him. Lieutenant Bradley. The file said: *'Stammer, voice gone for six days, persistent twitch in response to imagined bombs.'* A repeat of last time.

When Bradley came, he would knock twice, pause, and knock once more. Rivers would call him in. They would pour out the tea, rap the cups with spoons, and begin again.

He watched the taxi arrive. Two men got out – the orderly, and Bradley. Blonde hair, stooped shoulders – he didn't look up. Sassoon had looked up, had conquered his nerves with a deep-drawn breath, and taken the steps two at a time.

Rivers turned his pen over in his hand. He hadn't realised how much he would miss Mondays, 13:00. He went back to his desk, and opened the book of Sassoon's poems, looking at his friend's familiar, narrow script. *'For when I shut my eyes your face shows plain; I hear you make some cheery old remark – I can rebuild you in my brain, Though you've gone out patrolling in the dark.'*[8]

He shut the book, and waited for Bradley's knock.

1: S. Sassoon, *Sick Leave*

2: S. Sassoon, *Dreamers*

3: S. Sassoon, *The General*

4: S. Sassoon, *Sick Leave*

5: S. Sassoon, *Banishment*

6: S. Sassoon, *Song-Books of the War*

7: S. Sassoon, *Prelude: The Troops*

8: S. Sassoon, *To Any Dead Officer*

All of these poems are available at: bartleby.com/136/index1

END

The feelings we took don't work anymore.

Fingers and hairs, whispers and words.
They fall from the body in waves and clumps
As you clutch your head and shake.

In the face of true sincerity, it seems,
You crumble like a wall.
No hard feelings, no eye contact.

Hold you up against my chest and make you look
inside to the sum total of what I never told you.

Stay, don't stay, look away, my way –
The illusion fails. The screen is black.
I see you, now, sorry and honest,
And as pain becomes anger and the bruises start to fade,
For once, this once, you have nothing to say.

Your first gift to me, this mortal warmth,
Used and returned to its box, is yours again.

Two poems from the collection 'I Found Myself Swallowed'

ZELDA

In Africa,
the Arabs
and their eyes,
and the smell of ants…
The world became embryonic
and there was no need
for communication.

And then the end
at Easter.

Where will I find again
these months that dribble
into the beets of the clinic garden?
I'm becoming the flabby-legged huntress
of a corralled game
inappropriate
for a person of thirty.

Do you mind me writing this way?
I'm just searching
and it's easier with you.
It would be so decent
to make at least a stirrup cup
of this bloody mess.

I'm tired of rummaging in my head,
to make heads or tails
but try to understand
the throbbing
of these vaporous places,
and the way roads disappear.

Please don't write me about blame.
If atonement exists, it's occurring,
forgive me the rest of my part.

Is it fun in Paris?
Who have you seen there?
Is the Madame Pink
out at five o'clock,
do the fountains fall
into the framing of space
in the Place de la Concorde
and the blue creep out
from behind colonnades
through the grill of the Tuileries?
Is the Louvre grey
and metallic in the sun,
and are there lights
and the click of saucers
and auto horns blaring Debussy?

When are you coming?
You will be horror-struck.

LISA

When I was eleven,
God became a fool
and Jesus a prizefighter.
I've gritted my teeth
against the third name
for years.
Now I attach it
to everything –
apples and eggs
and the square root of x.
When it rains
I think of urination,
excretions of the nose,
a million a minute
shoot through me
like darts. *Ka-thud.*
I think
I was mowing the lawn
when my brain split through,
the sputtering halves
went round in circles
with the trees and everything.

VICTORIA MAITLAND

DUMPED: A DIARY

Defenestration

I thought the door was open and the window shut – a trick of the light, perhaps. I heard the former slam as you pushed me out the latter. As I fell I looked up into your face. You were pressing your forefinger into the space between your eyebrows. Your thumb was on your lip. I've lain for a while on this damp ground. The cold has seeped into my limbs and I am numb. I still do not remember landing. I sit and pick the harsh shards of glass from my flesh. They are a mountain beside me, and my skin itches from the scabbing wounds.

I haul myself up, dragging my broken body through the day. This is a new normality, a tiptoe where there used to be a confident tread: your footprints are everywhere and I am swaying between the cracks. Friends are tightrope artists on their lines, each slow step fusing bones. Your footprints shallow, and my bruises yellow.

By the time I crawl into bed my exterior is fresh, fixed, new. My organs are still displaced – my stomach sits too low in my torso and my heart skitters in my throat. There is an uncomfortable hole where my diaphragm should be. I hope the night will heal my pain.

The next morning I wake up falling.

Custard Skin

First thing in the morning, after dreams have lied and nightmares have twisted truths, my mind is soft and fleshy and turns to you. Memories roar, hundreds of them at once, and I see your eyes and your lips and your chest and your nose and your hair and your smile and your fingers and your stubble and I am consumed with you.

Eventually, the memories dim. My brain begins building up defences for the day and manages a thin crust: a custard skin. I hope it is strong enough to last.

Skin (i)

Sometimes, when I'm naked – in the shower, in between outfits, getting ready for the day, getting ready for bed – I think of you: the way you used to look at me in that perfect cliché (sexy and excited and shy, biting down on the corner of your bottom lip, dropping your eyes before you stare me down). I want to curl up in a ball and never have anyone look at me again.

The Baby

Grief is a newborn and I am its single mother. Selfish because it can't comprehend the existence of others, crying because every experience is one of the most uncomfortable things it has known, it draws the eye and captures all my attention. But I am post-natally depressed. I do not want to care for this creature, this thing born of me. It looks too much like you. Still I spend every waking moment attending to its needs. I cannot put it down and my arms are aching. Just as I'm drifting off to sleep it whimpers for more attention. I wake up in the night panicked that it's stopped breathing only to wake it as I rest my ear to its chest.

Trees

Memories like drying wood warp and shrink, but you are a forest and wood dries slowly.

Autumn

You are crisp October mornings, my nose cold on your chest. You are jumpers with holes at the thumbs and fraying at the wrists. You are woodsmoke and you are spiced oranges. You are a steaming cup of Earl Grey morning, noon and night.

Your scent is in all that is autumn to me. I hear you in crunching leaves. I taste you in the steam from my tea. When I lay in bed I cup my fingers around my nose to feel the ghost of your warmth.

Frying Pan

I lash my pain out at those who least deserve it – Mum, Dad, Sister, friends. Those who try to help the most feel the full force of my agony. It spits from my like fat from a pan and they wince away – rubbing at their wounds as if that can stop the pain.

Skin (ii)

On my forehead – chickenpox.
On my forearm – straightening iron.
Around my fingertips – teeth.
On my thumb – a tub of peanut butter.
On my shin – shaving.
Old scars have new wounds. You break open my scabs like a bent knee after a playground fall, blood clotting in the white socks like pain clots in the whites of eyes, curls up on tongues and bends fingernails into palms.

Moth and Bulb

Imagine a moth. It sits on a cool wall in a dark room. Perhaps it is sleeping, or maybe merely resting. The room is still and quiet. Suddenly, it is jolted into a frenzy, a flurry of beating wings, frantic through the air towards a single bulb of beautiful white light.

Then it is dark.

The moth rests back on the wall. Its heart rate is high. Its legs are tense. In its vision it can see green and yellow spots which only grow when it closes its eyes. It reminds the moth of the way the light filled the room, only for a second, filling in the cracks, illuminating everything.

The moth is pounding towards the bulb, stinging into the hot glass. The moth hurls its small brown body into the glass, recoiling, returning. It lands for a moment before the heat is too much.

The light is off.

The moth's feet are raw against the cool wall. Its wings are singed at the tips. Its body hurts. It is waiting for the light, an ache that will not fade.

It should be as simple as 'I am the moth' and 'You are the bulb' but it is not.

I am also the one in control of the light switch.

GREG MANTERFIELD-IVORY

COMMON LAND

I T IS A HOT DAY, AND SAMMY SITS IN THE BACK of his mum's Datsun
Cherry with his soft skin sticking to the vinyl of the seat. At the wheel,
his mum eyes herself in the rear view, adjusting her long brown hair.
She will not roll down the windows, she says, since it has taken her long
enough to get ready and she doesn't want the breeze to spoil anything.
So Sammy puts up with the heat, listens to Donny Osmond sing about
Puppy Love on the radio, and wonders where they are going. Eventually
they arrive at an open area of fields – common land. There is no car park,
but Sammy's mum edges through the open gate, and parks next to the
solitary car that is already there, waiting.

Sammy sees a boy standing next to the car, older than him, with
longer hair that hangs over his eyes like George Best. He is playing keepy-
ups with a football and ignoring the man beside him.

"Out you get," Sammy's mum says as she does a final double check
in the mirror. She opens the door and steps out on to the firm dry grass.
Sammy drags himself out from the car, peeling his sticky legs from the
seat. His shorts are scratching, he wishes he could have gone with his Dad,
wherever he was going today. The man from the other car walks over to
Sammy's mum. He is dressed in pointed brown leather shoes and bell-
bottom trousers. He wears a tie with his shirt and the sweat on his neck
seems to hover above his tightly drawn collar.

"Hi," he says to Sammy's mum.

"Hi," she says. "This is Sammy."

She motions down and the man smiles at Sammy, bending to his level.

"Hi there. I'm Charles."

Sammy says nothing.

"Say hello," his mum says as she lights a cigarette.

"Hello."

"Do you like football, Sammy?" the man asks.

Sammy nods.

"Well over there," the man says, pointing to the other boy, "is my son, Edward. He likes football too, and all sorts of other sports. I was hoping you two could play together."

His voice is different to the voices Sammy usually hears, more rounded and projected, like the man who reads the news. "Would that be okay, Sammy?"

Sammy nods.

"Well okay then." The man stands back up to his proper height. "Why don't you two run down to the other end of the field, by that fence down there, and make a goal. Here, you can use your shirts." He reaches down to Sammy again and removes his shirt, in one swift motion like a magician.

"Edward!" the man yells at his son, who barely looks up in response. "Go down there and play with Sammy."

Edward stares at Sammy, now shirtless as well as nervous. He says nothing as he boots the football towards the fence in the distance and begins to jog after it. The man gives Sammy his shirt back and gestures for him to follow, which he does without a word.

Sammy jogs at the same pace as Edward, but slightly behind. He clutches his shirt in his sweaty hand and feels the sun's glare on the soft pink skin of his back. After another few kicks of the ball, the pair reach the end of the field, lined by hedges and a short fence. Sammy turns around to look where they've come from and sees only two cars parked, like toys on a shelf. His mum and the man nowhere to be seen.

Edward takes off his own shirt and drops it on the ground. Sammy drops his a few yards away and instinctively knows that he is the goalie. Edward is older by a couple of years. The difference in their bodies is obvious even to Sammy. Edward is skinny, a chest like an ironing board and hair like a mop. His arms are disproportionate to the rest of his body, as though someone has formed him out of odds and ends they found about the house.

"How old are you?" Edward asks.

"Nine," Sammy lies.

"I'm thirteen in a couple of weeks."

Edward kicks the ball towards Sammy, who manages to stop it going in their rudimentary goal. He kicks it back to Edward and, after every save, waits for some indication that the pair are going to switch roles so that Sammy gets a turn taking the shots.

"Where do you go to school?" Edward asks

"William Roberts. Where do you?"

"Beachcroft, but I start boarding school in September."

"What's that?" Sammy asks.

"Boarding school? It's like prep but for older boys."

"Oh."

"Do you know what prep school is?"

"I think so."

"What is it then?" Edward shoots but this time Sammy lets it past him, so that he has to go and reach into the hedge to get it, giving him time to imagine what prep school is.

He returns to Edward, kicking the ball out to him. "I don't know," he admits.

"That's okay. I guess I wouldn't know either if I hadn't been to one." Underneath his bunch of hair Edward smiles at Sammy. "Prep school is a school where there are only boys allowed, and you live in the school. You stay in dorms with other boys, and they have the canteen where you eat all your meals and you have your lessons and play sports. And then at the end of term you come home and see your parents."

Sammy looks at him, trying to understand. "So you live at the school?"

"Yeah."

"Why?"

"Because Dad says it's better there."

"Oh."

They kick the ball back and forth in silence for a while, Sammy's head still spinning at the concept of living at school. How could it be better there? Trying to see an upside and find some common ground he says, "It would be fun to live with all your friends, at school. Where do the teachers sleep? Do they have their own room?"

"I don't know where they go. I guess some live in houses, but they're always around, even at night. If you're out of bed after lights out somebody will find you, it's difficult to get away with stuff."

"What do you mean?" Sammy asks, wishing he could go back to the car and grab the water bottle that had been rolling around on the floor underneath his mum's seat.

"I don't know. Just stuff at night, it's harder to do than I bet it is for you."

"Do you play football at prep school?" Sammy asks, trying to lead their conversation back.

"We always played rugby, not football. Have you ever played rugby?"

"No."

"It's easy, let me show you." Edward picks up the football with his hands and looks at Sammy. "All you have to do is tackle me and get the ball before I get past you and score a try. Okay?"

Sammy nods, feeling the afternoon heat burn even stronger. And now a football is being held in the hands of an older boy who goes to a different type of school, where they do things differently and don't even live with their parents.

As Edward runs towards him, Sammy vaguely tries to scramble the ball away, reaching to Edward's chest where the ball is cradled in one arm. But Edward sprints out of range and slides to the floor in the space between their shirts.

"That's three points to me. Your turn." Sammy wonders how one goal can be worth three points as he catches the football in his hands and resists the urge to kick it. Instead, he runs at Edward, who smiles as he charges at Sammy, colliding with him in a mass of boys' bones that collapses on the floor. Sammy now flat on his back, with Edward's weight on top of him. They both breathe heavily.

"Are you alright?" Edward asks.

"Yeah, I just – Can we just stop for a bit? I'm really thirsty."

"Me too. Let's just stay here for a minute." Neither of them moves for a while, Sammy with his eyes closed, trying to escape the heat. He wants to get up and go back to the car and his mum, but Edward is still on top and isn't moving. Finally he rolls away and they are lying still on their backs like lazy swimmers until Edward says, "Do you know what they're doing? Back at the cars?"

"I don't know. Talking about work? Mum said something about her boss."

Edward laughs a little. "They aren't talking about work."

"Oh. What are they doing?"

"They're fucking," Edward says, turning his head to see Sammy's reaction.

"Oh." Sammy says, trying to guess at the correct response.

"Don't you know what that is?"

Sammy shakes his head, unable to bring himself to look at Edward. He continues to look up at the sky. "You don't know much do you? Do you want me to show you?"

"Show me?"

"Yeah. It's really good. I mean, we sometimes did it at school, if you have a really good friend. Do you want to see?"

There is a lump in Sammy's throat, not just because he is desperately thirsty, but from the implication that he is worthy of an exclusive prep school activity. The dizzying sensation of being included by someone from another world leaves him eager to prove himself.

"Okay."

"It's really simple. All you have to do is take your hand and put it here."

They both stay lying on their backs, not looking at each other, as Sammy's small clumsy hands fumble around, following Edward's instructions. There is some unzipping and shuffling, and Sammy thinks he can feel wisps of hair where he doesn't have any himself.

After a minute or two his hand is cramped and stinging, but he continues to follow Edward's hushed guidance. Eventually Sammy senses a change, a snap in the once taut string and the sudden sensation of something he has never seen, and still hasn't because all he can see is the empty sky above. Neither of them looks down or at one another. Edward is quiet for a moment but Sammy continues. Edward lets out a deep long breath and then tells Sammy to stop.

"You're really good at that. Do you want me to—"

But before he can finish his request Sammy jumps up from the ground and starts running up the field, towards the distant cars. His bare back is itching from shards of stuck grass and he wants a cold bath, a shaded room, a cold glass of orange juice. As he nears, the door of one car opens and his mum gets out. She is barefoot, her red toe polish glints in the afternoon sun. The man then follows out of the same car door, a cigarette between his lips. Sammy glances backwards. At the far end of the field Edward is brushing himself off, zipping up his trousers. He picks up his t-shirt and leaves Sammy's on the ground.

Sammy tries to yell out to his mum but his mouth is so dry he can't make a sound. She bends down to the wing mirror, checking her lipstick and her hair, then spins around because she has seen him. Sammy, shirtless and sun-stroked, his hand outstretched like it is burning, runs to her, sprinting, tears gathering in his eyes.

He reaches her, shows her his hand. She looks at it. A webbing of something between the fingers, Sammy afraid and anxious, on the verge of tears. Edward kicks the ball towards the cars and follows it. The man stands smoking. Sammy waits for his mum to put her arms around him, usher him away from this place and tell him she is sorry for bringing him here.

She lets out a sharp breath and says to her son,

"Just get in the car."

AMELIA MARCHINGTON

THE PARASITE

Trial: Regarding the illegal termination of Test Subject #9MW6371

BEFORE WE BEGIN, I WOULD LIKE TO REMIND THE BOARD of their multiple requests to abandon the research in the early stages of the trial. By the end of the trial this particular test subject was wasting an inordinate amount of time and money. Regardless of how interested The Board may now be in this anomaly, they were not prepared to increase financial resources, nor provide more staff. Considering all the possible risks, it was impossible to justify continued research into this one small, insignificant test subject. I had no knowledge at the time of the interference with the subject's progress, and I terminated the test subject based only on the increasing security risk, and not to cover up the actions of the others on trial.

The first set of data was in accordance with of all of the galactic subjects we had created in the program. The initial planetary structures were of solid foundation, but this was by no means rare, or special. Within the expected rotation-span the predicted hydrating patterns emerged and subsequent floral cultures. Progress was fairly rapid at this point in comparison to previous subjects, but despite a slight increase in speed, no new flora or fauna were produced. We spent much time consulting the data throughout the experiment, and I can assure you that nothing new was recorded, and so nothing could have been lost. This charge is completely unsupported, and a simple consultation of our meticulously kept records is all that is needed. You will also note that the first and last reported sightings of individual species were kept on file. By the time the subject was terminated many of these early species had actually been eradicated. This unprecedented damage has been solely attributed to the outbreak of parasitic activity found on the test subject.

The parasites themselves actually occurred very late into the study, I think five billion rotations ago, but I would have to check the records. At first, they were very crude and unstructured, and took a very long time to progress. We cooed and clucked with glee when we observed their use of what they called 'fire'. It was almost as joyous an occasion as when they started playing with their little wheels! I take full responsibility for the lack of professionalism in the lab, and the informal reports from the time. It meant nothing and does not warrant such interest from the prosecutors. We had been cooped up in the office for several rotations, cabin fever had set in, and we were ecstatic that they had finally reached what is really a very meaningless benchmark. I hope the jury can appreciate that we were still fully committed to the study, and that it did not affect my work ethic. If only I could say the same for the rest of the staff, then we would not be here.

From that stage, it took far longer than we expected for them to progress, the other test colonies were incredibly successful in comparison. As I am sure you will notice, The Board requested an entire shift in the experiment. Instead of the normal procedure of focusing on all active life forms they insisted six of the twelve team members were assigned to record the parasitic activities exclusively. I appreciate that it was to assess this strange new life-form, but I still maintain that it was incredibly damaging to the overall success of the subject, as it resulted in a wide-spread negligence of the test subject's welfare. It is not a crack-pot conspiracy theory to demand an exact reasoning for The Board's actions. It is clear now that they are the guilty ones. They sabotaged the experiment from the beginning. They wanted my work ruined, my reputation destroyed, and me behind bars.

After this point, the parasites' slow progress turned into an active regression. It was completely unlike anything I had ever seen. We all now know that this was due to the illegal interference of the six staff members. I believe this was their first active role in the study, breaking away from their legal status as guardians and observers. They have stated on record that they provided a list of three simple rules so as to aid the cultural progress of the parasites. Whatever their real motives, the parasites' response was very destructive. It seems clear to me that they were trying to sabotage the parasite. They expanded on the rules, creating extra guidelines, which was then expanded into a completely untranslatable text. The interpretations of it plagued their entire existence, resulting in hundreds of unimaginably violent purges.

All their medical and scientific improvements were stripped away, replaced with rituals and blood-shed. There is nothing comparable in any of our records at all. It set back test subject #9MW6371 by many thousand rotations. Some say that during these dark times they were in fact carrying out their own research; they had become self-aware: developed an intelligence we could never have anticipated. The documentation was very contradictory and caused great debate amongst the team as we searched for a true meaning in their work. All that we can agree upon is that they were searching for their creator. This was an incredible new finding, the only thing that made the parasite special in any way. Now of course this revelation is nullified as they did not come to learn of their creation independently, but rather by the illegal interference of the junior staff.

Despite the unbelievable progress the test subject had made and that I had absolutely no explanation, I was assigned to another experiment. I cannot say exactly what took place during my absence, as the records are all classified. Even after I resumed my role over the experiment I was only allowed access to censored documentation. I have full security clearance on the project, which I founded after all. Even after repeated access appeals I was never allowed to see the original records. The staff that remained were all under oath, and were not allowed to provide me with any information about what happened in their own words. Many staff members were actually replaced. Only I and the six assigned to the parasite remained.

The violent actions of the parasite continued throughout the following rotations. However, within an alarmingly short rotation-span they caught up with the successes of some of our most intelligent test subjects. I watched as they split the atom for the first time, and I still hope my colleagues did nothing more than observe as well. Considering how slow their initial progress had been, I was astonished. I could not believe that such a rapid series of advancements could be possible. Now we all know that these achievements were not their own, and instead should be attributed to the illegal stimuli they received from the other accused lab technicians. I did not learn of their actions until my arrest. Until after our lab was trashed by The Board searching for evidence, after our records were confiscated, after we were all issued a life-ban from the project. And for what, may I ask? Did you think I'd be impressed that the subject had thrived under your care, without me? Was that it? That you wanted to prove you could do it all on your own? Without Mummy holding your hand?

The parasite continued to develop, facilitated by their deliberate destruction of many other life-forms. The violence escalated against their own kind as well as their planet. We observed as they remade themselves, and their habitat. The few remaining eco-systems were replaced with metals and plastics. They unified their kind via an omnipresent communications grid. They produced art of many media of spectacular emotion. They proved that they had mutated; they were capable of emotions and science of incredibly advanced levels, the likes of which we had never seen before. Nor will we ever again.

I believe now that it was at this point that the parasites had definitely been enhanced by the illegal stimuli. Their communication devices were so sophisticated that they began actively transmitting their messages out of their incubator, 'into space' as they dubbed it. It was clear that they had been pooling their resources to be utilised by their first research project. They had resumed the search for their creators, for us. We were naturally terrified, simply observing was impossible from then on. Their transmissions were difficult to translate, but they appeared to promise peace and camaraderie. We knew of course that they were innately violent beings; their destructive nature could not be controlled, merely disguised. Since their initial advances, they had promised in all tongues, with genocidal rituals, to send armies of the dead to their creator. It is true! They were entering their final phase: locating their creator so as to engage in an inter-galactic war with troops of the deceased parasites! I maintain that this is the truth, the only truth. I know it sounds absurd, but they really were going to send their dead to annihilate us all, and inhabit our lands. They knew we were out here, and they were coming for us.

We concluded that it would not be long until the parasite's growth could no longer be sustained by their birth planet. They continued to savage their habitat, rather than preserve its resources. It was clear that it could not sustain life for much longer, and their lack of care was further evidence that they had located us and were on their way. It would not be long until they reached full capacity and needed a surrogate planet, a new host, to infest. Whilst many will question this due to a lack of public awareness, I assure you that we alerted The Board of their violent plans, and they suppressed it all. There was no possibility of peaceful co-habitation. They killed all that was unknown to them. A single body of water was so large to them that they murdered or enslaved the strangers of the unknown territory, purely out of fear. It was as if they did not realise that they were all the same parasitic culture. They did not feel the heavy blade in their palm, and yet they all gripped the handle tightly, and together, they twisted it into the core of their planet.

Whilst the first illegal action that the staff carried out, without my knowledge, alerted the subject of our existence, they would have posed no threat had it not been for the later supply of the illegal stimuli. It is the only product capable of producing such a dangerous reaction in the parasite. I cannot stress strongly enough that it is the only possible explanation. The bizarre, unexplainable, and completely unprecedented behaviour of this one test subject must be attributed to the illegal stimuli, and they must be held accountable. The illegal termination, for which I have laughably been tried, must also be the responsibility of the other staff members on trial; as such drastic measures would never have been required had they not mutated the subject. That being said, as the senior staff member I understand that I should have ensured protocol was followed; that bureaucratic, meaningless formalities were adhered to, and the correct paperwork was filed. Unfortunately, due to my overwhelming fear of #9MW3671's potential violence, I decided that it was best to chemically terminate the entire test subject as quickly as possible, even if that meant resorting to highly illegal methods. Whilst the threat level may seem absurd to you now, at the time there was simply no explanation for the test subject's violent plans against us. I was acting of sound mind and was merely trying to ensure our safety against an uncontrollable parasite. I can only hope that you will appreciate that I had no choice, under the circumstances, and was simply doing all I could to protect us all.

ADAM MARIC-CLEAVER

PIGS

LET US TAKE A MOMENT TO THINK ABOUT GEMMA, who lives south of
the Thames and has nothing but a sofa and a refrigerator for company.
We shouldn't get too close. Gemma has to wash at her friend Freda's and
Freda is away. Gemma smells terrible. Let us put our faces to the cool
windows of the flat and peer. There is Gemma, lying on the sofa. She has
on loose-fitting clothes, all bland colours. Glasses squat on her nose, thick
framed. Gemma eases herself up, adjusting her glasses. It's time to eat.

She heads to the refrigerator, takes out a loaf of bread and a jar of peanut
butter and eats. This is done on the floor.

When she finishes, she puts the jar and the bread back in the
refrigerator and goes to a small room with a toilet in it. Then she lies back
down on the sofa.

This goes on for sometime.

Then, at 1 o'clock in the afternoon someday, someone knocks on Gemma's
front door. She rises, as ever, slowly and walks to the door, pulling up her
sagging jeans.

There is no one on the other side of Gemma's door. Well, let us be
frank. By "no one", we mean no one bipedal. There are, however, three
pigs, clean and patient, waiting for Gemma, scattered around the landing.
I suppose we could call them "someone". Three pigs must add up to about
one person. There is a logic at work.

The pigs don't notice Gemma for a while and she doesn't mind at all.
She is certain that someone is having a laugh at her expense. Perhaps one
of local teenagers or the pervert who lives upstairs. She doesn't want shit
in the flat, though, so stands in the doorway, legs apart. She risks calling

out for someone and regrets it when the pigs stop and begin to amble toward her. They advance, at first gently, but they pick up speed when they realize that their comrades are going the same way. Each wants to get its towel on the deck chair.

Gemma starts to close the door, but stops. She is as unsure of the reason as we are. This does not sit well with Gemma. She is one of those people who questions the motivations and actions of characters in film, wondering why Such And Such did this and his mate with the scar didn't do this or why a female character did not do Such And Such given that he was clearly gagging for it. It therefore troubles Gemma that she does not close the door and allows the pigs past her into her home. She looks at them as they nuzzle the sofa and scratch the floor. She closes the door. One of the pigs shits.

It is sometime later and the pigs are quite at home. They are taken with Gemma's lifestyle; the peanut butter and the sofa and the long periods of showerless freedom. Gemma has even invested in a tray which she has taught the pigs to crap in, though it needs constant emptying. The pigs seem grateful though and snort contentedly when the house is clean or whenever Gemma comes in from work or the shops with a fresh jar of peanut butter. She has to kick them out of the way going to the fridge and then rubs their heads on the way back to the sofa.

Let us not have any illusions, though. Do not think for a minute that Gemma is fond of the pigs. But once she sorted out the issue of them crapping everywhere, there was no reason for them not to stay. She has asked Freda what to do. Freda didn't know, having never had pigs in the house.

"You're the expert," she told Gemma.

As a result of her apathy, Gemma has tried only once to remove the pigs, by placing a jar of peanut butter outside her front door. But the pigs, in spite of having eaten nothing but peanut butter for the past two weeks or so, are unmoved by the jar. Gemma kicks one of the pigs, a little half-heartedly. It nuzzles her leg.

The pervert upstairs has come to ask about the snorting noises. He says that they are keeping him up and while he knows that Gemma's personal life is none of his business, he was wondering if there was any way of the noises not occurring every night. He says all of this to her breasts.

Gemma leans on the doorframe and tells him that she is keeping three pigs in her house and asks if he knows anything about that. He says no.

"I've never kept pigs before," he says.

It takes him a few seconds to realize she is asking why the pigs were in the block in the first place.

"Oh... no idea."

Gemma thanks him, assures him that the snorting will be kept to a minimum and turns back into her house, feeling his gaze move down her back like a cold raindrop.

She shuts the door and heads to the fridge. The pigs are massed there, rubbing themselves against each other in excitement and snorting.

"Shut it."

The snorting continues. A kick.

"Shut it."

Silence and then louder snorts than ever.

Gemma gets down on all fours. The pigs are intrigued. One snorts and gets an eye full of spit for its trouble. It shuts up and they all look Gemma directly in the eyes.

We can't be sure what the pigs see in those eyes and we shouldn't speculate. But all of them stop snorting and they watch the eyes as Gemma awkwardly crawls backwards, towards the sofa.

And then, one day in the middle of summer, there is no more money. Everything saved, everything earned from odd jobs and borrowed from friends, is gone. The peanut butter and bread supply is meagre. Freda is pregnant and her generosity has dropped with the rise of her stomach. She has to provide for two now.

The pigs are huddling around Gemma, grunting for food. They may well have been food themselves, but for Gemma's lack of an oven. Our heroine is reading a newspaper and trying to work out what jobs she could do. But there is nothing.

She hoists herself up off the floor, using the pigs as support, and walks to the sofa. She lies down and recites the names of everyone she knows. The list is not long. Gemma's immediate family are all dead, as far as Gemma is aware at least. She hasn't made an effort to stay in touch and has still managed to attend four funerals.

She gets so desperate with the names that she starts listing shop owners who she half knows. A butcher's sign appears. Something and sons. A little further away than Gemma usually ventured, but she knew one of the workers there

She looks at the pigs. Would he prefer one alive or dead? What would fetch more?

The pigs turn to look at her and their black eyes settle it: dead. She couldn't hand one over, knowing it would die, having it look back at her as it was lead away. It would have to die here.

She selects a pig at random. None of them have names and Gemma silently praises herself on this, as names would have made this harder.

The pig is compliant as she pushes it onto its side. It is used to Gemma's violence.

It doesn't even flinch when the first blow is dealt to its head. On the second it squeals and tries to stand, but a foot clamps it down. Another kick. Another scream.

This goes on for some time.

When Gemma is done, she drags the pig toward the fridge. It doesn't fit, so she leaves it out for the evening. The room is fairly cool. She just needs it there until morning. She hasn't yet thought how she'll get the pig there. Maybe she should bring the butcher here and he can take it over.

She looks back at the dead pig, trying to feel for it, trying to connect herself to it and she's almost there and then she feels hunger cut through her thoughts. There's no room for any other kind of pain.

Gemma walks to the sofa and lies down. It is only as she is just about to fall asleep that she realizes she doesn't know where the other two pigs are.

Let us take a moment to think about Freda who, concerned with her friend's well being, has come to Gemma's flat and got in with the spare key she has.

Gemma is out, as Freda can't see her shoes.

Freda goes to the sofa and kicks off her own shoes. She can smell those pigs. The tray has been emptied, at least.

Freda rubs her inflated stomach and looks into the plastic bag she's brought. She's realized that there is some food she can spare and she's brought it as an apology for her being selfish when Gemma needed her more than ever.

There are noises near the fridge. They've been there all the time, but Freda hadn't thought about them. They are soft, wet noises.

She looks up and sees two of the pigs eating the carcass of another. They are nearly done.

Freda gets up, unsure whether to pull them away or call for Gemma or run. So for a long time, all we can see through the glass of the flat window is a heavily pregnant woman watching animals survive the only way they can.

ERIN MICHIE

STAINS

YOU INSIST WE GO THROUGH THE FOREST TODAY. You say a schoolmate mentioned it was a shortcut. I know it isn't. If anything it's a longer route, a meandering trail which loops the school's fenced perimeters, adds an additional five minutes to our journey. And I can tell you're fibbing by the lisp that slips into your speech, the way you tug at the drawstrings on your coat to make the hood concertina, like puckered lips, to conceal your face. We take the trail anyway.

I exhale clouds of bitter cold as I grip a cigarette between my teeth, and fumble through my pockets for a lighter. Deadfall snaps underfoot as you you tiptoe around behind me, stealth your middle name as you sneak through the undergrowth. I pretend not to notice the crunches and carry on patting down my pockets, fondling clumps of lint and foil gum wrappers with my fingertips. A smile creeps across my mouth, and it almost causes the cigarette to fall. Any minute now and you'll pounce.

There. A weight, soft and small, collides with my lower back. It would be unnoticeable – unless I'd been waiting for it. You give me a brief shove, attempt to drive me a step forward, before you snatch the pressure away and try to dart past. But you're slow and I'm fast so it's easy to snag your collar. I yank you back into a headlock whilst you struggle, bleat a complaint at being outmanoeuvred or trapped under my armpit. Either way, it makes me laugh, which riles you more. So I give one more squeeze then let you loose. I light up.

Heat blooms inside me, and the taste of nicotine spreads within my mouth. I take a moment to swallow the warmth before letting it trickle, spiral out of my nostrils. In my periphery you pull exaggerated expressions, mimic my showy smoking style. You think I can't see you, but I do. I know all your tricks.

I didn't always. I didn't know you until six months ago. Sure, it was easy to find out the facts, like your name, age, hair colour, eye colour, blood type. I didn't know who you were, though, not really. But in my arrogance I believed I'd taken the necessary steps to prepare. I'd sourced references and recommendations, filed the appropriate forms, danced to the government's organ grinder tune until at last I was certified, told *yes, you can legally care for another human being. Yes you can cope.*

When the social worker knocked on my door, a bundle of black clothes and anger clinging to her arm, I wasn't so sure. I almost sabotaged it from the very start. You were fresh from the funeral, still steaming hot. I was lost in the haze of a hangover, my skin slick with the previous night's sweat, and my ears clogged with wasp-buzz tinnitus. You were a blurry weight of responsibility and my shoulders sagged.

As I led us to the living room, I'd stood too tall, walked too straight, trying to appear a trustworthy kind of sober. I held my breath in an attempt to avoid expelling telltale whisky fumes, while the social worker settled you in. I'd made myself appear all sharp edges to overcompensate for my slips and slurs. And then we were left alone, and we shuffled around one another with the stilted, silent awkwardness of strangers. Your arms stuck straitjacket-tight to your sides, like you were terrified to touch what wasn't yours. A mirror of misery. Then my stomach rumbled, empty, and you loosened at the sound, became less tin-man. It proved I was human, at least.

Eggs? I asked.

Pancakes, you replied.

Lemon? I asked.

Raisin, you replied.

I'd never made pancakes before, and also never seen someone eat so many in one go. I thought it a thumbs up from some higher power, that it meant I had a handle on the whole business of cooking and providing. I said I could cook pancakes for every meal if you liked them that much. You seemed happy enough with this proposal, considering.

But it was never going to be so easy. A few days later you exploded, imploded, created black hole destruction. You went through every room of my house, sweeping each fragile thing to the floor. Smash, crash, bang. The sounds soaked through my headphones in a distant echo, happening elsewhere, another person's problem. I was concerned with lyrics and melodies and the next pop-trash hit that would fund our food. It was when you appeared in my office doorway, arms outstretched like an accusation, that I realised what had happened. Cuts crisscrossed your hands and feet, and you trailed streams of red along the cream carpet. It had seeped into the wool faster than spilled Shiraz. A part of you looked proud.

I hadn't expected to perform this kind of first aid. The tweezers, the bandages, the antiseptic – they were intended for bike-riding incidents or tumbles from park playground equipment. Not a child's rage. I was a shambles, shaking fingers and shaking words, adrenaline and misdirected aggression. I'm ashamed that I shouted. The antiseptic or my anger stung too much for you to do it again.

We settled into a routine after that. I found myself reciting eight timetables and prompting answers to five sentence comprehensions, ironing polo shirts and creasing small-person school trousers more than I thought humanly possible. Each morning I twisted laces, *the bunny loops around the tree trunk,* into double knots for you. And at supermarkets you'd piggyback ride around the whole shop, clinging to my back, your arms wrapped around my neck, coiling close in an anaconda grip each time you thought you might slip. People stared. You weighed a lot, but I didn't mind.

Yet the truth was, beyond the basics, I didn't have much of a clue. So I looked on websites and chat forums, bought books and subscribed to podcasts. I even joined *First Time Fathers,* some community centre group which turned out to be a dozen or so self-congratulating, wannabe middle-class men who sat in a Kumbaya circle and took it in turns to flash photos of their children from the plastic flap of their wallets.

They spewed a lot of rubbish in those meetings. However, once their quota of pretence and preening was spent, they did offer some tidbits of advice. Suggestions of fresh fruit, organic vegetables, balance and sustenance of the soul were the main bullet points. 'Put the effort in,' Phil or Kevin or Henry told me, 'and you'll get the desired results, tenfold.' Like you were an investment, a time-share in the Maldives. The sentiment was solid though. Anything that might help us both out.

Of course, as we'd stood in aisle twenty of Asda and I suggested the adjustments, these little betterments to ourselves, all you wanted was pizza, crisps and chocolate. You were angry that I'd try to change you. And we argued, debated and bartered, tugged at a packet of Monster Munch until we were both flushed and security started sidestepping their way towards our struggle. In the end, we compromised with Kettle Chips. There'd be plenty more compromises as time went by.

Just this morning I found a school letter on the kitchen counter, weighted by my favourite coffee mug, declaring that Parents' Evening would take place this time next week. You'd placed the letter next to the microwave, maybe because you realised that I still struggle to cook proper meals, opt for easy-way shortcuts where I can, impatient for instant results. But we're learning.

We've almost made it to the school's entrance now, and I look over at you, a blur of bright colour in your red raincoat, which is female and two sizes too large, and your gross green backpack which is tearing at the seams. You chose them yourself, so I let you think they're cool. In your backpack is the reply slip. I've ticked the box to say I'll go, I'll be there. I signed my name and slid the response between the pages of your school planner. And as I sit and listen while they tell me what you've done, or not done, I'll know what really matters.

Watching you race ahead toward the school gates, tripping over tree roots and calling for me to chase you – these are the moments that matter. These are the moments that stain me.

I stomp out my cigarette and widen my strides to catch up. You never win, but I think you like someone there to catch you anyway.

When I get home I'm going to call them. I want you to stay.

JAMES MORTIMER

BOB

I AM MARRIED TO AN ALIEN.
Although we mustn't use the 'a' word. It encourages racism in society, and is generally frowned upon. Instead, we say, I am married to a person of 'other origin', or, at a push, an 'extra-terrestrial'. The word 'marriage' is a fallacy as well – the term 'life partner' is more accepted in polite company. I once used the term marriage at a gathering on my life partner's planet, and I found myself locked inside the children's Papier Mâché Doom Cannon for the rest of the evening.

While engaged, or 'indefinitely bound', as they refer to it there, we decided that, although there are no genders on my life partner's planet, he was going to be a male. We call him 'Bob'. He calls himself Bob. Everyone calls him Bob.

My husband, a term which he has no objections to despite its gender connotations, is quite short in stature. Short, you understand, by human terms. He's actually quite tall, on his planet. He's grey, with a head like an upside down tear drop, and eyes like Carmen. Only bigger. And just black. He only has pupils at certain times, which can be a bit disconcerting. His pupils form when he's either angry, bored, or sexually aroused. You understand, this made reading him on the first date quite difficult.

He has a thin body, skinny arms and legs, webbed feet, and a 'bit of a tummy', although that description from my mother has never gone down well with him. He eats only twice a day, and receives parcels of Neurothine (pronounced 'Neurothin', I've since learnt) in the post every two months from his own planet.

I don't know too much about his past. He's the first one in his family who has been able to travel back home. The name of his planet can't be pronounced in human terms, so I won't bother trying to spell (or, more accurately, draw) it. Apparently his parents managed to recover the original craft that their grandparents arrived on Earth in. They landed in Nevada, as I learnt after I'd already made several jokes about Kurt Cobain. They'd been trying for decades to get the craft back. I think there was an issue with the paperwork.

I've only been to his home planet three or four times. To me, everyone looks the same, but he thinks all humans look the same too (which is a *very* flattering thing to be told over the dinner table at Luccio's). His people are all slightly different shades, their skin slightly different tones, their eyes varying in the smallest ways.

His great-grandparents had, I understand, a tough life on Earth. They were the first extra-terrestrials to arrive here, and so, naturally, ran into some difficulties with the authorities. Bob's parents, who are lovely, although slightly conflicted about him, their only son, marrying a human, adopted a unique lifestyle. His mother makes wigs, which she wears, usually alongside a pink apron and stick-on earrings, and his father works in insurance. Or banking. He has a bit more of a tummy than Bob does. He wears a shirt and tie, although no trousers fit him. It's the lack of an actual waist that has caused problems.

Despite his unorthodox upbringing – his parents were the first to learn 'American', for example – Bob is quite a traditionalist. He's very proud of his family and his upbringing, and likes to go back home as often as possible. I've promised we'll go there for our next holiday. I don't need injections, or a passport, and I take sleeping pills for the journey so Bob doesn't have to blindfold me to stop me knowing his planet's location.

Bob, having been fluent in American by the time he was three years old (Earth equivalent), had no problems in society. He told me, when we met, the story of the time he was walking down a street, and a policeman held a gun at him. It turned out he was holding it at the human behind him. People are far too preoccupied to notice Bob. Bob does no harm to anyone, anyway. He had a rebellious phase during his teenage years (Earth equivalent), and once hijacked his planet's real Doom Cannon, but doesn't that happen to everyone?

It's a Tuesday evening.

I've just got in from work – I work for a TV network, I'm the Equalities Officer on their latest science fiction production – and am sat on the sofa. It's only a small house we have. There's a parcel sitting on the mat. I place it on a side table. It must be Bob's Neurothine. When his people realised his great-grandparents were trapped on Earth, they began to develop the drug, a way to allow them to survive in our atmosphere. It's poisonous in its pure form apparently, which is odd, because it's such a pretty shade of green. But in small doses it's fine. Bob injects himself with it every other weekend. It always makes him a bit drowsy, bless.

The door opens. It was a bit of hassle moving the door handle further down the door, but Bob needed it. It's degrading, having to jump up to reach it. I turn round, and Bob walks in. Being a traditionalist, Bob doesn't like wearing clothes. No one on his planet wears them. In fact, Bob told me that the word 'clothes' would roughly translate to 'despicable garments' in his language. However, despite society's acceptance of Bob, it was initially noted by our neighbours that walking around naked – even with *that* body – wasn't totally okay.

Bob is wearing his silk dressing gown. It's the end of the day, so it's come slightly undone. It always gets like that. It fits him perfectly. We had to go to quite a few shops looking for a suitable despicable garment in a child's size (Earth equivalent). He sighs. His tiny mouth reverberates slightly. Bless. He shuts the door behind him, and I turn back to look ahead of me.

His bag is thrown down by our cabinet. He places one hand on the back of the sofa, and flings himself over the top. He lands next to me, and rests his head by my shoulder.

I ask him if he's had a tough day. He tells me I know how it is. I do. Bob's had a lot of tough days recently. He's essentially doing two jobs since his colleague left. His boss is trying to find someone else, but he can't. He doesn't know why. They're the most popular realtors in town.

I put my arm around Bob's shoulder, and my hand rests on his upper arm (Earth equivalent). His skin doesn't feel like mine does. That's one of the reasons he likes me, he said. I feel soft. (The other two main reasons he likes me, so he said in his most recent Valentine's Day card, were my warm personality and something else I can't divulge here.)

I tell him I was going to make fish and chips (Bob is a vegetarian, but not a vegan). He's happy with this. We sit like this for a bit longer. I never feel like Bob needs to hear about my work. I feel he just *knows*. He can sense if I'm unhappy about something, then he'll ask.

I stretch my legs out on the sofa, and Bob adjusts accordingly. He kisses my neck.

The clock chimes when it gets to the hour. I've always hated that chime, but it reminds Bob of home. Apparently, the centrepiece of his town (Earth equivalent) was a giant clocktower. He had his first kiss at the giant clocktower, with a girl (Earth equivalent).

It's getting later in the evening.

Bob is sitting in another dressing gown with slippers on, ones my parents made for him for Christmas. It was a lovely thought. They tried to replicate his name, his actual name, in cross stitch, and very nearly didn't fail. It's a cute gift. Bob looks cute in them. He's borrowed my reading glasses. Apparently, the Earth atmosphere can affect sight slightly in people of other origin, so poor Bob suffers sometimes. He's in the kitchen, working.

It's late, I tell him. Maybe we should go to bed. He tells me soon, he's just got a few more pages to finish. He's looking through an application. Despite their rarity, Bob's boss is 'too busy' to look through them. Bob thinks his boss is a bit of a dick (Earth equivalent), and although I've never met the man, I'd probably have to agree. Bob finds his job quite stressful, so I try to be supportive, although the stress of it sometimes stresses me out too.

He tells me there's a message from Sandra on the answerphone. Aww, I say, it's been ages since we heard from her. She married her personal trainer in Ohio, and then moved to New York when he became the face of a famous underwear brand (I had to explain the concept of underwear to Bob), and she became the face of a depressed housewife. After some therapy, we got a postcard from Barcelona to say she was feeling better.

The answerphone message says she is in town and wants to come visit with us. I will ring her back tomorrow.

I leave the kitchen, giving Bob an affectionate rub on his small shoulder as I walk past. My eyes look to one of the pictures we have on the wall. We visited Disneyland on one of our first dates. The children there wanted to take pictures with Bob, but Bob, who had a cold at the time, wasn't too keen. We enjoyed the rest of the time though. It must have been only the third or fourth time we'd met. We met, by the way, in a cloakroom. A rack collapsed, and we accidentally half fondled under fallen duffel coats. After awkwardly parting, we awkwardly bumped into each other again standing in line up for cupcakes the following day.

Bob didn't even like cupcakes. Apparently he'd just felt that was where he had to go. My mother always says it must have been fate.

Our wedding ceremony was a quiet affair. His parents couldn't come and so it was just my mother and father, a few of my friends and a few of Bob's colleagues, including the homophobic woman who works in the cafeteria. Apparently we had 'changed the way she saw life'. She also had new glasses that day. I didn't know if she was trying to be symbolic.

I arrive in the bedroom. Events from the day appear and dissolve in my mind. Then something jogs my memory. I wonder if the Neurothine parcel has moved. I didn't mention it to Bob. He normally puts parcels by the bed to sort them out the day after. I rise, and walk down the corridor.

I don't make it as far as the sitting room. As I walk past the kitchen, I look in through the door. Bob isn't sitting on his chair. He's on the floor. Some sort of seizure. Hands flailing, up and down, three, four times. Legs kicking wildly. Saliva, oddly coloured, running from his mouth. Is that what colour his saliva is? Why have I never noticed before?

I run to him, I grab his shoulders. I try and speak to him, urging him to stop. Is there a recovery position?

Pupils appear in his black eyes. I doubt he's sexually aroused. Is he angry? Maybe there's another reason his pupils appear. Maybe he told me. Maybe I've forgotten. How could I forget this? He tries to say something. I listen closer. He tries to point instead.

His short, spindly, finger – how many times have I held that finger? – is pointing to the unwrapped parcel on the desk. I grab it. The inside is bathed in green. Such a pretty shade of green. At the centre, a broken vial of Neurothine. Poisons splutter out. I look to Bob.

He's covered in the green, and blistering.

MY SO CALLED LIFE

It hurts.
It *hurts.*
It hurts and I am sobbing.
It hurts and I am sobbing and I am swearing and I am drinking and I am
    dancing and
I am going to *love* that boy. The one in blue.
It hurts and I want my mother's belly to bind me to myself but I don't have
    her I have
You, boy in blue. So give me a toke, these lungs are mine to break while
I suck on a cigarette become the best part of me, all that's *vogue* and *rogue*
    of me,
It glues my wormy insides together, we need and feed each other
Until we both glow in the dark. It is safest in the inhale
And I try so hard to hold my breath ... But I don't have time, the club
    closes at four so
We need some drinks and need pierces my eardrum like a truth that makes
    me retch but
Jaeger's on offer so I'll have a double *and can everybody shut up because I*
    want to make a
toast.
Here's to the labels that never warned us. To the fig trees we rolled into joints.
    To waiting
for the
drop and missing the starting pistol. To the one who got away, to the one we
    ran away
from, to
the one who might have been Our one, to laughing about it later, to crying
    about it late at
night, to
the fact that it's not facebook official and to absolutely never getting fucking
    over it, to
you,

Boy in Blue. To my house.
It hurts like an ache.
Like an ache in my chest that drills deeper and deeper and ow. Ow. Ow
      Ow OW OWW-
DJ ORDERS
US TO SCREAM BUT I AM AREADY SCREAMING WE ARE ALL
      SCREAMING LISTEN TO
US PLEASE,
it hurts.
I think the stars are so much further than they seem.
And I am not Claire Danes.
And I am here and I am hurt.

LIAM OFFORD

IN THE DARK

ONE TOOTHBRUSH ISN'T ENOUGH FOR A HOUSE.
This becomes obvious as I plunge my toothbrush into my mouth to combat the day's meals, whilst a trickle of excess toothpaste oozes out of the tube I have so recently abandoned. The sharpness of the toothpaste dances around my tongue as the toothbrush thrusts into the tiny tributaries of my teeth.

I allow my right hand to direct the brush while my left hand lingers on the basin. I tap my fingers in the correct order. Thumb, ring finger, index finger, little finger, middle finger. Thumb, ring, index, little, middle. I simply have to do it this way. It isn't a matter for debate.

Toothpaste tastes sour after a while.

I spit it out into the sink and watch the foamy white substance trickle into the tap water, spiralling for a moment at the bottom of the basin, threatening to pull away from the sink and jump at me, affronted at being spat out. I can see why people close to death are said to be circling the drain. The toothpaste claws at the sides of the plug hole, clinging on for dear life, clutching at its last few moments in the light. Then it slips into the drain, disappearing into the darkness. A mix of plaque and minty freshness and bits of that cheesecake I shouldn't have had before bed falling into a deep abyss I don't want to think about.

I rinse off my toothbrush quickly, bristles all gnarled and wiry since I always brush too hard, and place it back on to the shelf. A battered, battery-powered sword against all forms of tooth decay. It looks lonely so I put some dental floss next to it so they can share some hygienic company. Maybe I should get another toothbrush, a back-up. One really is too few.

I flick the bathroom light off as I walk through the corridor into the dining area. I stagger past the empty pile of blankets and cushions in the corner, not really looking at it. A yawn attempts to worm its way out of me, climbing up from my stomach. I try to stifle it a second, I don't know why, but the yawn wins, as always.

Bed is a tantalising prospect. I've been staying up much too late recently. Why do I do it? I have to get up every morning to feed the dog anyway; staying up late just means I don't get any sleep.

I glance at my watch, analogue of course, as the second hand ticks by. Clocks and watches really are depressing things. They are nothing more than permanent countdowns, reminders of approaching deadlines and eventual destructions, of heartbreaks and break-ups. Time is such a loathsome thing, a mistake; it's a self-imposed restriction and limitation upon humanity that's been impossible to escape since the instant man erected the first sundial. It's far too easy to feel the seconds, minutes and hours building on each other, mounting and climbing, spiralling upwards behind you until virtually all your time in the world has gone and you're left with nothing more than one fleeting second ahead of you. Then that too passes and suddenly you slip out of the world as easily as a wisp of smoke fades unseen into the clear, empty air.

Still, as I reach the threshold between the dining area and the hallway I see the second and minute hands of my watch move in sync as it hits 10:23. I have conquered time today, so there's no use worrying. I'll be in bed at a reasonable hour, plenty of sleep. Smiling, I turn off the light in the dining room and step, alone, into the dark hallway.

… Something's wrong.

This feels off. There's something I don't like. The darkness isn't right. It's hiding...What? As I step into the hallway and move towards the stairs I feel my unease rising whilst the darkness just sits, heavy.

I reach the stairs and thrust my hand out blindly, searching for the railing, hoping I don't find anything else. I reach and reach, and still I find nothing. Surely the bannister cannot be this far away? It was a matter of a few inches. I must be lost, teleported somewhere by this malicious darkness, placed in some empty, barren, lightless hell: hurled, on my own, into oblivion. Then my hand clasps the rail and it becomes apparent this is not the case.

It's still dark though. I can't see anything, but the fear is still creeping up on me, the fear that something's amiss. I rack my brain and think and think and think. Trying to figure out what's wrong. I can't make sense of anything as a colourless blanket is draped over my mind, creating an abyss where my thoughts should be, ink-like patches blotting out my brain.

I squeeze the railing firmly, and plant my foot on the first step. I can feel the soft red carpet beneath me, though I can't see it. My muscles tense and I consider running up the stairs as quickly as I can, desperate to reach my room, praying it will be a haven, a cocoon where the jet of night won't intervene. I don't run though. Fearful of making too much noise, of being heard by something I can't see, I take another breath and slowly begin to climb the stairs. One at a time, treading softly as if the carpet were eggshells on a frozen lake. My neck starts to feel cold. I feel the nauseating sensation in my back that comes when someone is standing behind you, casting a shadow on you. The stairs start to feel a little steeper, and my room a little further away. What could be casting a shadow in this darkness? What malevolence is lurking, watching me, one step behind? Trailing, waiting. Panting and snarling at my neck, holding back its cruel laughter while I climb and climb.

I used to like the night. It's a time for exploration and discovery, not trepidation. For bravery, reaching out into the dark and finding something unexpected. A time where you don't have to see or be seen, when the other senses can flourish.

But now? I don't want any of that. I don't like this darkness; this crushing, inescapable, universal blindness. I want to be able to see, see that there are no monsters or fears hidden in the shadows.

The top of the stairs finally arrives at my feet as my heart ricochets around my chest. Slamming into my ribcage in an increasingly frantic drum beat. Surely whatever's out there, in the dark, will hear me.

Head bowed, I trudge towards my door, still walking carefully on that fragile carpet, scared to make any more noise. The menace at my back grows and growls. I can almost feel a claw formulating out of the pitch black behind me, scratching at my neck. I stop and turn. Nothing. I see nothing.

Standing still, looking behind me for a moment longer, I sniff the air, wondering if there is a foul scent, something that might indicate why I should be afraid. Nothing. I smell nothing. Just clean, bland air enters my nose. The dark has somehow robbed me of two senses. I try to remember how this hallway should smell. I don't know if hallways have specific scents to them, but it's a redundant thought; the black fog is still clouding me, and I can't remember the smell of anything. And I still can't figure out why everything feels wrong in the first place.

It does feel wrong though. I realise just how alone I am and the desperation to reach my room increases as I turn around again and take another step into the darkness.

SQUEAK.

I veer back as the chew toy I have just stepped on makes an infernal noise, a vicious alarm, calling all demons and devils out of the dark towards my presence. What a way to go, ratted out by a toy. I close my eyes, not that it makes a difference, and wait for the hell to come. I wait and wait, but nothing materialises of my misstep. I wait still, but I am alone in the dark. Just a few steps from my room, my heart's crashing solo has lost its rhythm in the empty silence of the night, I feel it skip a beat.

I swallow and note the faint taste of toothpaste on my tongue. The cool freshness of the mint washes over me for a second as I continue on down the landing, a momentary respite. I begin to relax, and the dark doesn't feel so close at last. My haven is near. Perhaps I'm being silly. After all, this isn't a horror story, it's just my life. Why should I expect anything to pounce on me, as if I were some poor defenceless animal? It's arrogant, to be honest, to expect something to crash into my life like this. What would a monster want with me? What would anyone?

Then I arrive at where I think my room is. I reach a tentative hand out and the refreshment freezes and shatters as I feel my door hanging ominously ajar. The dark sweeps in again, encasing me whilst dread poisons my insides, coursing through my body. Darkness around me and bleakness inside.

My room is not safe. It doesn't offer any protection. It isn't a place for me to hide and wait for the light. The darkness infests my room as well. Inescapable.

There is nothing else to be done, so I push forward my door, ready to meet whatever morbid fate the ceaseless black has for me. I step into my room and flick the light switch, and at last the haze lifts from my head and I recall that pile of empty blankets in the corner of the dining area, and I realise why everything feels wrong.

I turn to my bed and see the beast, lying there, tail thunderously thumping against my pillow. A weak laugh tumbles out as I look at my tormentor.

'Spike, you silly dog, you shouldn't be in my bed. Go downstairs!'

'Ruff!' Spike barks back.

I trudge over to the bed and lie down on my back next to the dog, eyes fixed on the ceiling: empty except for the light shining in the centre. The light looks down on me, so bright that I have to shut my eyes momentarily. Underneath the impromptu spotlight my stomach coils in fits and screams in an attempt to wretch up my shame. I wonder if the light likes this, lighting me, alone, for the whole world to see. Laughing at me for being afraid. I hate that light, I'll buy some different bulbs tomorrow.

Afraid of the dark? It's childish, it's pathetic. For a second I'm glad there is no one here to see my failure. What's wrong with me? But I know what's wrong. My eyes open to watch the fingers on my left hand tap against the air: thumb, ring, index, little, middle. I can see it, the disgusting tan line on my ring finger. I almost wish the darkness was back.

My eyes close again. The light and the line and the loneliness too much. At least it's normal to be lonely in the dark. I can screw my eyes shut and wait for the clocks to speed past and accumulate time behind me. Dreary seconds and minutes and hours can slip by and I can stay here without any problems.

But this isn't true. I sit and I stay and I refuse to open my eyes, but the misery still swirls around, cruel and isolating. I become all too aware I'm on my own again, catapulted into a new home and new life. There are plenty of places to try and hide in the dark but I can't escape that phantom around my finger, the ghost of my ring and my marriage.

I can feel my future hanging over me, alone and still. My future knows I have to spend the rest of my life afraid of the dark, with no-one to protect me if there is a monster lurking unseen. A life with nothing left presses down, squeezing me until my eyes open.

Spike is standing over me instead, head cocked to one side as if that will somehow help him understand what it's like to be alone. He's a ghost too. The puppy I… *we* bought years ago is gone now, replaced by this beast. Spike stands over me, as if I were his dog. He intends to stay with me, to hunt and haunt me, dragging my old life, my memories, into my future. This is worse than the light; as the dog looms over me I wish I really was alone.

Spike thrusts his tongue down towards me.

I think to recoil but I allow myself to be assaulted with canine kisses. An illuminated blend of fur and tongue and whiskers crashes into my body; I feel ridiculous again and replace the incessant tapping of my fingers with pats and strokes of my dog.

I hug Spike and he nestles into me, a ludicrous wrestle of affection. He blocks the harsh light above and I'm in the dark again. I'm in the dark but my dog is with me, and a new future begins to open up. A future that can let go, one that isn't heavy with the divorce and the dark. Spike doesn't care about old memories, and as my new life drifts on ahead of me, unburdened, I can't wait to follow it, with my dog. I laugh as he continues to kiss me, noting his acrid breath as it makes an unwanted intrusion into my nose.

I should really see if it's possible to get toothbrushes for dogs.

LILY OZANNE

SPLIT (MILK)

THE FLUORESCENT LIGHTS ILLUMINATE EVERY CORNER of the shopping centre. This is not the clean, nourishing light that sneaks in through the windows but a cold, dirty, artificial light. A light that can betray you. Yearning to catch you out from the moment you step through those sliding doors. Staring at you and everyone else with that scrutinizing gaze. Waiting for you to make a mistake, to trip up, to show what you are really doing down there below.

'Thief! There! Thief!' It will scream, and its minions, those rabid bulldogs better suited to a cell then a salary, will come pounding out of their window box. Racing down the aisles, they're practically frothing at the mouth at the thought of taking you away.

So that's why you have to know what you're doing. Because you can't afford to be locked up, just like you can't afford all these things the mouths at home are screaming out for. Though it's more the eyes than the mouths that get to you. And they don't actually scream very often. Which makes it worse. Because you know how they suffer. What they need. There's no one else but you to give it them.

You buy what you can. But the rest. The rest you steal. You have a choice, of course you have a choice. But do you?

But no use with pointless questions aimed at no-one who listens. On to more practical matters.

The three rules of shopping (on a tight tight budget) are as follows:

1: Choose your outfit carefully. Nothing too showy. Nothing too shabby neither though. Definitely no tracksuits or hoodies; the staple of a stereotypical shoplifter's closet. Flat shoes. So your trip up is less likely to be a literal one. One bag, only big enough to fit your wallet.

It's only for money though, nothing with your name on – that way even if you're caught you might still have a slight chance. The coat's the most important thing though. Go to a charity shop. Buy one of those big puffy ones, the biggest one you can find. Pull out the lining, makes more room for essentials. Otherwise you're gonna get way too puffy quickly and attract some unwanted attention. Then you can either cut slits in the bottom of the pockets or sew squares onto the inside of the coat, or both. Of course, some coats are designed like a maze of pockets. Unfortunately they tend to be the expensive ones which people aren't gonna give away very often, so that's not really an option here.

2: Know your surroundings. Never rob on a first visit. Use that as a chance to scope out the place. Map out exactly were those tiny flies are buzzing above the heads, work out which corners are the blind spots. It's not a rule, but you like to only go for the big name supermarkets. With independents, you can't really be sure. Family businesses often need the pennies just as much as you do. Somehow, I doubt Mr Asda or Ms Tesco's children know about it if a few items go missing from their stores. In fact, they're probably part of the reason you (and the rest of this country) are in such a dire economic mess. Oh, and don't go to the same place two weeks in a row, like a farmer rotating fields each year. It could be dangerous for you if one patch becomes over ploughed.

3: Know your aims. This is where the list comes in. You might think you can remember it all without a piece of paper, but if you forget something, what then? You gonna go back in there to get it? It's best if it's written down, for everyone's sake. You should know exactly what order you're getting things in as well. Nowadays, you always split your lists so as not to forget what's going where.

So, now you know the basics, let's give it a whirl. Start this week like any other, grab a trolley from the racks outside. You notice there's a new security guard, you can tell because you've got to know them all by sight over the years. And you don't know this one. But you know what you're doing, so stay cool. But, remember, that could be a problem. Abort mission? Not an option. Breath. You're just an ordinary shopper, just like everyone else in here. Apart from that as far as you're concerned everyone else in here is an off duty policeman (or woman). Remember, a conscientious busybody with good eyes is just as dangerous (possibly more) as a bored employee or a watchful lens. So keep your eyes peeled: three hundred and sixty degree awareness. Is. Crucial. At. All. Times.

You know exactly where everything you need is. You will zig-zag your way through the shop with the utmost precision and assuredness.

Never look at the flies buzzing above you, but stay alert to them; you never know how many eyes could be looking through them at any moment. Straight at you. Is it paranoia? You know you're the one they're looking to catch. No small fry but a big fish; a professional, practiced pincher. Someone who does this week in, week out.

Breathe. You're just a normal shopper, just like everyone else in here.

Four toothbrushes, toothpaste and a bar of soap hide inside whilst the other hand turns a jumbo pack of shampoo and conditioner, as if the low price tag isn't all you needed to know about them. They go in the trolley, so does a multipack of own brand washing detergent, the non-bio stuff.

Next, to the pasta aisle and you slip two packets of spaghetti into your pocket. But the one kilogram of penne will have to be paid for (for obvious reasons). Into the trolley.

You're getting into the rhythm, now, as you graze along the fridge and freezer aisles unencumbered. Then on to fruit and veg, none of which can be secreted away. The proper price must be paid: they go to the trolley. It's okay though, you've saved a bundle on the cheese and butter. Half and half on chilled meats.

Feeling generous when you come to condiments and spreads. Not to mention there's a silly old biddy hovering behind you, seemingly unable to make up her mind. Seemingly harmless. All goes into the trolley when it becomes obvious after a few minutes of waiting that she's gonna be stood here for quite a while.

Breathe. You're just an average shopper, just like everyone else in here.

You're gonna have to make up for it somehow though; your coat is not as full as it should. Milk? You're managed it once or twice before. Feeling lucky! Hell, why not even grab the eggs? Who cares if a few break? They will have been free of charge, after all.

Walk calmly to milk and creams, at the end of the bakery.

Or maybe you're not so calm...

Your hand must be sweating because the first semi-skimmed you pick up slips right through your fingers and crashes to the floor, spilling everywhere. Strange. That's never happened before, not really sure what the protocol is for such an incident?

'Clean up on aisle 8 please,' pronounces the tinny speakers as you stand and watch the white liquid spread across the linoleum floor towards your practical footwear. If there were cracks it would be dripping through them right now. Drip. Drip. Telling on you. But that's not what's happening. Not here.

There. You see it: the tub perched on your bedroom floor. Catching the drips from the ceiling. Calling to them and reassuring them that it's okay to fall. You see the bucket in the front room and the one in the kitchen. They've not been there long, but they'll be there a while longer before you can afford to fix the holes. Maybe by then the house will be full of them. You see it right before your eyes. The whole floor made up of containers of all types and sizes; the bath perpetually full of dirty rain water. The drip drip drip now an incessant background to your life.

For a while, you thought you'd got away from it all, you really did. You were nearly out, nearly graduated. But then mum got caught, not for the first time, and she went away this time. So you had to come back, get back to your old tricks. Do these things just like when you were 14. Apart from it's just for them now, not for you anymore. You don't need this any more. You know better. But...

'It's alright. Don't you worry about this, just carry on with your shopping. Please,' instructs the smiling assistant knelt at your feet.

You didn't even notice her arrive; you've been standing motionless, as if stunned, staring down at that spillage, not even noticing it disappearing before your eyes. Too long. Suspiciously long?

Maybe you're not feeling so lucky today. You decide to pay for the milk and eggs and get out of there before anything else can go wrong. Before you forget.

Breathe now. You're just a typical shopper, just like everyone else in here.

You apologise and pick up another milk and place it in the trolley. Then wheel off to get the eggs, which follow the milk.

You're not feeling well. Need paracetamol. It'll be easy enough to get into your teeming pockets as long as you keep your back to the apparently friendly pharmacists' window. But it does mean walking back across the aisles you've already crossed off your list. You cave to temptation and the ache rearing up in your stomach and are on your way, practically before you've make up your mind. That's fine; indecision is unwise in this game, you've just got to move with your usual confidence.

Bakery. Fruit and Veg. Freezer. Fridge. Spreads. Pasta. Toiletries. Pharmacy. Easy. Peasy. Lemon. Queasy.

You were right. In it goes without a hitch and you sigh in relief that you've nothing left. Only to pay and get out of here.

You smile as you make idle chit-chat with the middle-aged lady at the till and wish that this place would hurry up and install self-service already. She probably doesn't even care what you've got in your pockets. She wants to get out of here just as badly as you do. To her family. So you thank her, smiling, and walk away, bags in hand.

Breathe. You're just a standard shopper, just like everyone else in here.

The finish line is in sight. You completely ignore the scowling security guard beside them, as you grin foolishly at the happy prospect presented by those sliding doors. Just a few more steps. And you're through, breathing in the free air of the parking lot. But nothing is really free, is it?

A hard hand lands on your shoulder and you have the urge to run. 'Excuse me there; mind if I check your bag, please?'

What do you think?

I split.

Shampoo and Conditioner	Toothbrushes and Toothpaste
Laundry Detergent (Non-Bio)	Soap
Penne Pasta	Spaghetti
Chicken	Cheese (Cheddar)
Chips	Butter
Peas	Ham
Potatoes	Ketchup
Apples	Mayo
~~White~~ Bread	~~Nutella~~ Chocolate spread
Eggs	Jam

Milk?

MOLLY PEARSON

SKIN

THE FIRST TIME I ACKNOWLEDGED TO MYSELF that I loved you, a patch of my skin blistered and died. The remnant was rough to the touch, the dull crimson of poison ivy, and crinkled like a first-degree burn. It was on my left arm near the elbow.

It's funny in retrospect how little I minded. The disease seemed innocuous at first – a speck, a nothing, an excuse to wear a long-sleeved shirt. I thought it would clear up in time. Thousands before me have told themselves the exact same lie. Case in point: the addition of cancer. Division and multiplication at the same time on a cellular level. The subtraction of life. We all think it will clear up in time.

We met up for a drink with our mutual friends. My suggestion. A bar half-full of neon light with car seats for chairs, antiquated jazz playing loose through speakers that looked as if they'd been salvaged from a skip. I sweated through the jacket that covered the scabs on my arm and talked to you in words I barely understood. Your replies were sound and motion; my senses, trying to follow them, spilled like my drink across the table and dripped onto the floor. The xylophone rattle of a dropped wine glass, the stickiness of the bar under my fingers. Yesterday's rock stars sulked on the walls. Under the hot blue light your eyes were large as a ghost's and shining.

That night was the hottest of the year, so hot I couldn't sleep. I plugged in an electric fan and put it on my bedside table, turning the dial to maximum power, but even cooled by the frost-giant blast of its breath my dreams were feverish. I chased you through crowds, buildings, the maze of my mind. Sometimes I knew who you were at once; sometimes I didn't. And all the while, the steady whirring of the fan settled, lifted and resettled on me like a mosquito. All the heat of the world was in my skin that night.

The next morning when I woke, I found that the sickness had spread. The little rough patch by my elbow had more than doubled in size, creeping down towards my hand and upwards to my shoulder. It was harder now, and a darker red, almost the colour of liver. When I tried to bend my arm, the joint resisted. I was starting to calcify.

I sent you a text.

I booted up my computer and scrolled through encyclopaedias of different ways to die. Searching. Searching. No skin disease had symptoms like mine.

I sent you a text.

I took a picture of my arm and posted it online. I waited for comments.

Haha very funny

Wtf??

Time waster.

I sent you a text.

Then I bit the bullet of my lower lip and dialled. You were not in at the moment; please leave your message after the beep.

Later the scab on my arm cracked and began to weep, a pale, viscous fluid that clung to my fingers like oil. I covered the wound with a bandage and went to bed, but the infected skin crawled until I couldn't sleep for the itch of it. At last I got up and switched on the light. The bandage was damp and the disease had spread far beyond its edges, covering the whole arm and half of my chest. When I lifted the damp white pad to my nose it smelled hotly of decay. My sheets were slimy with white secretion, littered with a faint patina of hairs shed by the dying flesh.

Exhaustion and fear drove me to my knees. Slumped on the carpet, I realised that I was saying your name over and over like a an incantation to some god.

I booked an appointment with my GP. Yes, it was urgent. On the pristine surface of the doctor's desk, my fingers looked brittle enough to snap. She inspected my arms with a microscope, ran her gloved hands across my ridged red ugliness.

'I can't see anything wrong,' she said.

Nor could the skin specialist she referred me to. In his mint-green consulting room I heard the word *hypochondria* for the first time.

'What's the matter with you?' I said. 'I look like something out of an Eighties B-movie!'

'I'm terribly sorry,' he said, his politeness shallow as the puddles on a bathroom floor. 'I wish there was something I could do.'

Outside the clinic I took off my jacket, baring my arms and shoulders to the harsh sunlight of a thousand stares. Pedestrians filed past with their bags and dogs and children, but their eyes slid over and off me, blankly indifferent. Were they really blind to what was happening to me, or had they simply chosen not to see?

I went home and opened my medicine cabinet. Sudocrem lay uselessly on the surface of the skin for hours, unabsorbed, until I wiped it off. Aloe vera stung like cold fire but did nothing. Vaseline was a waste of time.

I took pills. Benadryl, bicoloured antihistamines and the tiny white moons of hydrocortisone tablets, which you could snap in half to speed up their effect. I took them one after the other and lay on my bed and made paper aeroplanes out of the brochures the doctors had given me. The title of every leaflet was prefixed with *psycho*. I supposed I ought to be grateful. A hundred years back, they would probably have dissected me and put me in a jar. Ethanol. Formaldehyde. Glutaraldehyde. Phenol. All those elixirs of death with their pretty little names.

It's funny, but I've never mentioned love to you. We've never discussed it. Our relationship is built on small things, in-jokes and song lyrics and moments snatched from our separate lives, tiny specimens in dozens of jars. Love isn't life, but it fills the spaces in between.

I called you again, and this time I left a message. Then I went downstairs and made myself a shot. I can't remember what it was: some kind of schnapps that smelled like cinnamon. That didn't matter. It was time to look.

The mirror I had hitherto ignored was framed on three sides by wall, its bottommost edge perched above a sill that grew bottles of beauty products like toadstools. I plucked them one by one and threw them into the bin.

Moisturiser.

Mouthwash.

Deodorant.

Soap.

Why not? I didn't need them any more.

The mirror agreed, but when I gazed into its silvered heart I saw I hadn't changed. I was a little paler than usual, my expression anxious and drawn, but my reflection showed no trace of the disease that was consuming me, inside and out.

I still held the shot glass in one mutilated hand. A cool trickle ran down the side of my face as I tilted my head back and poured it into my eye. The pain was almost unbearable, and through my tears I saw the room break apart into a thousand glittering facets. Agony buzzed in my ears. I filled the glass again.

The hands of the clock moved as if showing me the way. Time's taste cloyed on my tongue like an opiate. My reflection swam in the side of the schnapps bottle. The scales were creeping up my neck now, over my ears and chin; soon they would cover my face. I touched my blistered cheek. 'Why can't anyone see it?' I whispered. I was miserably drunk. 'For fuck's sake, why can't anyone *see?*'

The next morning you knocked on my door. I answered it in my dressing gown, thrown on over yesterday's clothes. My heart was racing, I was covered in sweat and I could hardly stand. Leaning against the doorframe, buckling under the weight of your gaze, I said nothing; watched you try to turn your wince into a smile. Relief like warm soapy water. Then you spoke.

'What've you done to your eyes?' you said. 'They look really bad.'

Wordless, I went to the kitchen and found a ball of steel wool lying in a Gordian knot on the draining board. Following, you found me kneeling on the floor, bubbles of fluid seeping from the cracked and darkening skin as I scoured my hands and face as if I could wash this cancer away.

You caught my wrist. 'What's happening? What are you doing?'

'I don't know,' I said. 'I don't know.'

LAURA PHILLIPS

THE GIFT

"I'M VERY SORRY." HE RESTED HIS HAND UPON MY SHOULDER. "I expect your mother has about a year. It may be less." He'd seen us through the last two years and now the consultant was preparing to give up on us. His finality squeezed the air from my lungs.

I didn't tell her she was going to die. I tore up the hospice booklets they gave me and refused visits from the chaplain. The doctor cooperated, unwillingly. You are very sick, he would tell her. But not too sick, I would add, tightening my fingers around hers. Life was only bearable when we were pretending.

*

The need to drop the baby rippled through my muscles. My arms extended in front of me – the baby as far from my body as possible. My thumbs pressed into the gaps between her ribs. Rib, thumb, rib. I could feel the soft skin of her back beneath my fingernails. How easy it would be just to release and spread my palms to the ceiling. Her chin rested weakly on her chest. Her legs begged for me, kicking, violating the space between us. Her black eyes blinked at me. So like mine, so like mum's. I couldn't meet that gaze.

Her blood wouldn't stay inside her, we couldn't keep it in. We sat for days and weeks and months, a grotesque drip protruding from her arm. It would take doctors an hour to find an open vein in the maze of empty ones. We passed our lives in those rooms, bags of foreign black blood passing through her skin, mixing with her own.

When we left the hospital on those dark evenings, we convinced ourselves that tonight the blood would stay put. If it was a nose bleed we could manage. I could tut and hand her the tissues. It was when blood poured from her bowels into the toilet bowl that my body tightened. We made our familiar journey to the same A&E, to answer the same questions from the same doctors. Me with my big alien belly pushing a wasted woman in her wheelchair. Their eyes questioned me. What is the point?

Only twice in those months did the blood escape through her mouth. The last time she vomited streams into the first thing I could reach – a blue pot she had had as a wedding gift. She served potatoes in it. The blood was thick like jam. Her body convulsed over that bowl. I wanted to grab her by the shoulders and shake her back to life, to cut open our palms and press them together, my blood nourishing hers. She retched a final time and then was quiet. She was limp over the bowl, the ends of her hair dip dyed black. I took the bowl, trying not to notice the solid masses. Bits of her insides were coming away. She looked up at me, her body damp, and half smiled.

*

Three months after the consultant's prognosis, I told her I had a gift for her. I wrapped a red ribbon around my middle, a bow tied an inch above my bellybutton, and presented myself self-consciously. She was in the day clinic, legs raised on a footstool, head resting against a pillow. I was sure they never changed the covers on those things and I had to stop myself from snatching it away. My mind was full of germs.

"Darling, that's wonderful. My first grandchild." She picked her hand off her lap, tugged at the ribbon, and squeezed my cheek against her fingers. I pushed my face into her cool palm. "A little bit of happiness for both of us. Finally." The fist in my intestines unclenched for a moment, basking in her smile. *For you. It's for you.*

*

My midwife appointments were short. She disapproved of my preoccupied manner and lack of partner. I didn't mind. "What are the chances of this baby being premature?" I asked.

*

Her blood was the enemy and the battle exhausted her. Platelets and haemoglobins. Cancer. Neutrophils and paraproteins, light-chains and plasma cells. Cancer. Lesions and dialysis. Cancer. She was words to me now. Alien medical lingo that I obsessed over night after night, waiting for her to take breath after breath.

*

The day she died, she woke up unable to breathe. She lay in bed awake and wheezing. I laid next to her, vainly pumping my asthma inhaler into her mouth.

"Darling…" she said, her voice threadbare, chin resting on her chest. "Can you lift my head?"

Her muscles were giving up. I placed my hands either side of her face and pulled her head upwards, forcing my eyes into hers. She had burst a blood vessel in her left eye. It engulfed her pupil, red and demonic. It was coming out of her eyes now.

The paramedics arrived and snapped an oxygen mask to her face. Eased by the gas now in her lungs, she insisted on dressing. We shut them out of her bedroom and were alone in our ritual for the last time. Her body was too weak to lift and zip and stretch. I held her skirt as she held my shoulders and lifted in one shaking foot at a time. I stayed crouching for a few seconds, my cheek pressed into the cotton and my arms around her calves. The baby, eight months now, was kicking my insides. Taunting. Oh, to crawl through that skirt and back inside of her. We three, safe inside each other, dying together like Russian dolls. I rose to pull a t-shirt over her head.

"Come," she said. I brought my face to hers and she kissed the wetness of each eye, one hand on the baby. "Be okay."

*

I laid the baby on the table and stared at her. She terrified me with her accusatory looks and violent little body. I lifted her into the crook of my elbow to dress her. The clothes were fiddly on my fingers and I tried not to touch her skin. I didn't want to leave any more impressions. I transferred her into the buggy. She gasped as the fresh air brushed her face as I bumped her over the threshold and into the world.

The handles felt strange under my hands as we walked. My fingers wrapped awkwardly around the plastic and my grip kept slipping. My feet stepped out of time with the wheels so that we intermittently lurched forward. We walked in our clown routine for an hour, me out-of-synch with the buggy, glad that she faced away from my failure. When we stopped at the hospital entrance, she emptied her lungs, throwing fists as I kissed her face. She screamed as I backed away. People were staring now and I turned to run.

I'm sorry, you were for her.

JAKE REYNOLDS

PUNCH

In the back garden she notices
that everything here happens in bolts
and grins mid-gulp, as the birds
hurtle above and look like they feel
the quiet between all things.
She recalls the science class fact
she will never shake: that we
are never truly touching anything,
that nothing reaches back.
There is more black in her eyes
than ever before, as a pseudo-profound
boy tells her his room is the comfiest in the house.

HOTLINE

He plays back his sister's videos until he reaches a moment
he thought only existed as a photograph: she cartwheels
on black sand in her boyfriend's clothes, like a wave.
He sees the frame the picture came from, frozen at the apex,
her nimble limbs, the wind imprisoned in the shirt folds,
more alive than anything. With glass-dark eyes
he checks the time and dials Mystic Megan's Spirit Guide Hotline.

I wish you could see her, he says, wearing clothes
that aren't her own! I wasn't sure when I called last night,
but I know now, I know I'm right, it all lines up, listen:
the jewellery was hers, but the body never was.
She played a game and slipped her rings onto someone
before the wave's crest formed a shadow.

Megan listens in her mystic way and says she sees her,
alone in a remote log cabin on a tiny island owned by a widow
who grows vegetables in a patch out back.
He nearly has a heart attack: of course. She always loved
the idea of her own little allotment, and excursions
to remote places, it works, it fits, it's even quite nice
to be alone in knowing.

THERE WAS

there was a short time
there was a time when we
were counting
(courting,
in an obscure and
secret way)
the things that exchanged between you and me like

1) punches:
as we passed in
the corridors
on our shoulders
covered by uniform sweatshirts
but shook through me
as if there was nothing cushioning your fist
as if I were naked like
in the nightmare everyone has
at least once
about being naked
when everyone else's bodies are covered
by a uniform sweatshirt

2) looks:
when no one else was watching
shyly given
dart to/dart from
when the other one
wouldn't see

<u>3) the times we saw each other outside of school:</u>
three;
twice inside
once outside
the village surgery.

> when I got home each night
> I logged onto MSN
> awoke the wires and signals
> that connected me
> undeniably (albeit
> without much confirmation)
> to you
> to talk about

1) girls who watched
The X Factor
with leggings on
(who I thought I was better than
because I listened to The Smiths
and wore skinny jeans)
2) how one day we'd leave
that rain-falls-hard-on-a-humdrum-town town
separately but kindoftogether
because we would both be in the city
sharing the same Tube trains
maybe even sharing the opposite seats
eventually,
> like if time glitched
> and we found ourselves
> overlapped in a double exposure –

like when you said
'I hope we meet
after school is over.'

FOUR WAYS IN WHICH LITTLE RED COULD HAVE MET THE BIG BAD

I

THE WOLF GROANED. HIS BELLY WAS TOO FULL. No longer soft and warmly satiated, but heavy and leaden and suffocating. An acidic gurgle rose up in the back of his throat like a warning that he'd gone too far. He knew he'd be up half the night clutching a bottle of Pepto with clammy paws.

Granny was easy. The old woman hadn't a chance to blink before she was halfway down his throat. He'd swallowed her whole without even having to glare his big bad eyes or bare his big bad teeth. He wandered around the house afterwards. Had a glass of milk, admired the dusty family photographs, and borrowed a John Grisham he'd been meaning to read. He was checking his reflection in the hallway mirror – lest he forget the time he found a bit of wool lodged between his teeth halfway through a blind date – when he heard a *rap tap tap* at the door.

The wolf peeked through the lace curtains, ready to bolt if it was that awful lumberjack again. But it was just a kid. He'd seen her around the cottage before, always pedalling away on a battered blue bicycle and shouting for Granny to watch her. She carried a wicker basket in one hand and a can of soda in the other.

He thought about bursting out the door snarling and barking and chasing her back into the woods, but the idea seemed rather gauche – he had just eaten her grandmother, after all – so instead he crouched behind the paisley sofa and hoped she'd just leave the basket at the door. But the kid was persistent, pounding on the door and ringing her bicycle bell and calling out 'Granny!' in between slurps of Coca Cola.

It was then that the wolf began to worry. The kid wasn't going away and he didn't know that he could get out of the house without making a scene. Even if he did scare her off, there was no guarantee the lumberjack wouldn't come to her rescue, and the wolf wasn't sure he could outrun him this time. He looked around wildly, searching for something, anything, until his eyes fell on a pile of dirty laundry. He had an idea. Feeling rather clever, he pulled on the first things that fit, crept back into the bedroom, and dived into the bed.

'Come in,' he'd called out in his best falsetto. The kid had taken one look at him and asked where her granny was. 'I *am* your granny, dear girl. Don't you recognize me?'

'My grandmother's not a transvestite dog,' she'd snarled.

His grin faded. The kid was right, of course. He looked ridiculous. His ears were sticking out of the little plaid cap, the gown stretched disastrously over his haunches, and his breath still smelled of vapour rub and must, not to mention those awful butterscotch sweets grannies always keep in their pockets. But he didn't know what to say. There was really no good way to tell someone you'd devoured their relative. 'I was hungry,' didn't seem to cut it somehow.

It was hard to be a wolf and it was getting harder every day. Nobody cared if you had a protein deficiency or that your fur fell out when you went too long without a granny or two. Nobody believed that you hadn't meant to blow down the little pigs' houses and that you just had hay fever and very powerful sneezes. Nobody understood, not even the other wolves, who laughed if you combed your fur or wore scarves in winter or listened to books on tape.

He hadn't wanted to eat the kid, really. He'd tried to reason with her, but she just screamed and hollered and spilled her Coke all over the rug. She fought going down too, all thrashing elbows and gnashing teeth. Even now, he could feel her unmoving weight like stones in his belly, refusing to digest and threatening to burst angrily out of his chest with every rumble and burp.

He sighed again. Yes, it was hard to be a wolf.

II

Red threw a stone into the river, exhaling a whirl of grey smoke as it skipped across the water's surface. She had her first cigarette two years ago on the anniversary of her father's death, crouched down behind the truck so her mother wouldn't see her. This was cigarette number seventy-two. She never had to buy cigarettes either; even now she was still finding her father's Luckies – hidden in the cupboard behind the jar of olives that nobody really liked, tucked into a shoe box at the back of his closet, and even taped to the underside of the driver's seat. The first time she presented her father with a pack dug out of his sock drawer he told her every man had secrets and keeping them was the only way they got women. Maybe women kept secrets too, though, because Red was sure her mother knew he smoked, and always knew, but she never said a word.

She'd shared that first cigarette with her sister Marjorie. They sneaked out of the house while their mother made dinner and lit it with the wooden matches Marjorie kept tucked in her sock. 'A girl should always be prepared,' she said. Marjorie was two years older than Red and knew most things. She kept telling Red to breathe the smoke into her lungs, not just hold it in her cheeks like a squirrel.

Marjorie blew smoke rings into the sky. 'Sometimes I think I'm too much for this one body.' She said things like this from time to time, when only Red was around to hear.

'What do you mean?'

'I don't know. I feel everything. I *want* everything. Like one day I might gobble up the whole world if I'm not careful.'

'Maybe you're just a little wild,' Red said. 'Like one of the wolf boys.'

Marjorie sighed. 'Maybe, Red.'

The wolf boys lived on the other side of the river. Nobody but those boys ever crossed the river and it was said that they were born from the brown churning water itself. They never went to school or to church on Sundays either. They smoked in the alley behind the 7-Eleven and set each other's tails on fire with the cigarette butts. They dared each other to lie between the train tracks when the six o'clock came thundering over them and then they'd hitch rides on the caboose. They were free, in a way that Marjorie and Red were not.

Until that December, when Marjorie left home with a wolf boy of her own. His name was Alexei. He had dark brown hands that tapped restlessly on the kitchen table and a coat of dark brown fur that grew heavy and full in the winter. Marjorie was jealous of it until one day he bought her a coat of her own, a cape that just kissed her knees and with its thick crimson wool. 'Just like you,' Marjorie scribbled on the back of a postcard. 'Red.'

Marjorie returned in August with a swollen belly and lines beneath her eyes. 'That's what the wolf boys do,' their mother had said. 'They eat you up until there's nothing good left.'

Red slammed her hands on the table and said it wasn't fair, but her sister only sighed. 'It's how they are, Red. They get to be wild. We don't.' And Marjorie wasn't, not anymore.

Red tossed another stone but this one sank into the dark water.

'Hey sweetheart,' a voice said, coming from behind her.

Red whirled around. It was a wolf boy. She'd seen him before, maybe even spoken to him. It was hard to tell; there were so many of them. He seemed to know her, in any case, and chatted on while she turned back to stare at the river.

'So what do you think?'

'What?'

'Do you want to come home with me?' His smiled toothily, pink tongue darting over a chipped canine.

Red exhaled another puff of smoke and pulled up her hood. It was crimson, lined with dark brown fur.

'Sure.'

III

Red sang softly under her breath as she picked her way through the field. It was September and already the grass was dry and brown and prickled between her toes. She checked her watch. She was supposed to be at her grandmother's by now, just like every Sunday, but she'd been taking the long way there since last July when Granny said she was 'getting a little chubby.'

Red looked up. Far away, on the bank of the river, she thought she heard something (or someone). And something (or someone) made her run towards it.

It was a wolf. His belly was heavy and misshapen, held together by a line of crude black stitches that stretched from his throat to his stomach. What little fur still covered his blotchy pink skin was thick and clotted with blood. When Red reached out to touch him he yelped pitifully and yellow tears oozed out of his big black eyes.

Red hesitated. Her mother always said not to talk to wolves. But this one didn't look scary, shivering all over with his tail between his legs. No scarier than her granny at least. 'What happened to you?' she whispered.

'The lumberjack... He found me sniffing around the chicken coops. He cut me open and filled me up with stones.'

'If you let me, I think I can help you,' she said.

'Please.'

Red half-carried and half-dragged the wolf to her grandmother's house, behind the cottage to the shed, where he collapsed onto a pile of straw. She emptied his belly of stones and she sewed him back together as carefully as she could. She stroked his ears while he gobbled up Granny's casserole and she tucked her cape around him when he began to snore.

And every day for a week she crept into the shed while her grandmother watched *Wheel of Fortune*, stealing crackers and bread crusts and anything that wouldn't be missed. Every day for a week she applied creams and salves and anything that might lessen his pain. Every day for a week she pressed a kiss to his cold black nose and promised she'd be back.

They talked sometimes. The wolf told her that he had six brothers up north. 'They're all so big and so bad,' he told her. 'I never was. Mom always says that one day I'd be the biggest and the baddest of them all, but...,' he gestured to him himself, 'I don't think I ever will.'

'You will,' Red said. 'You just need a little time.'

On the eighth day, as Red bicycled to Granny's she heard a great commotion. Her grandmother had found the wolf. The old woman dragged him out of the little shack and slammed the handle of her broomstick into his head again and again, shouting at Red to go get help.

But before any help could come, Red threw herself onto her granny and shrieked at the wolf to run. He did, and he didn't stop.

A week later Red picked up a paper at the corner shop. The headline read, 'Brave girl saves grandmother from the big bad wolf.'

Red smiled, and somewhere the wolf was smiling too.

IV

Sometimes Little Red Riding Hood thought she saw the wolf of lore: a black brush of a tail disappearing around the bend and then the crunch of leaves or the snap of a stick when she thought she was alone.

Sometimes the Big Bad Wolf thought he saw the fabled girl with the cape: a swish of scarlet darting across the forest floor with a trilling voice that called out words he had never heard and songs that the birds never sang.

But they never met. Not really. Not yet.

EDWARD ROSE

FULL ENGLISH

I COOKED MOSTLY. JOHN JUST POTTERED ABOUT – slipping his arms in and around me to snatch bits of bread out of the toaster every so often as I fried the bacon and eggs. My sister had bought us a smoothie maker from Argos for Christmas. It sat and growled at us as we scurried around in front of the morning sky outside the window. On the radio they were doing a feature about men who had been "traumatized" by witnessing their wives give birth. The show was dragging on by this point and I was surprised by the amount of call-ins. John was by the sink, sipping his tea and listening as the callers went on, gushing with their stories.

"Could you fetch the marmalade, John? It's just in the fridge…" I turned to look at him when he didn't respond.

"Oh yes, right." He said and set his tea down.

I had put three rashers of bacon into the pan and the meat was starting to whiten, areas of pink rising and going pale in the snapping oil. I looked down at the kitchen towel where I'd put the last rasher and it was gone. John came back over with the marmalade and reached between my stomach and the counter, grabbing at the drawer handle. His hand brushed against my apron. I stepped back, he opened the drawer.

"You wouldn't've happened to see what I did with that last bit of bacon, John, would you?" I said. He picked out a knife and opened the jar of marmalade. It popped. The radio seemed a bit too loud. The oil in the pan continued to spit and sizzle beside me.

"No, love. What've you done with it, then?" I looked back down at the sheet of kitchen roll, blank apart from the moisture the rashers had left on it. "I don't know…" I murmured.

We spent the next few minutes looking around the counter tops and checking the floor for the lost rasher. They started playing Cilla Black on the radio, "You're My World" was the song. It was still a bit loud; her voice seemed right in my ears as I got flustered scouring the kitchen for that bit of bacon. I could smell the rest of the rashers cooking, knew that the eggs were going cold on the table. I don't know why, but John decided to cook them first. Just at the end of the song, I happened to lift up my foot to check the sole. Sure enough, the rasher was stuck to the bottom of my slipper. I started to giggle, though I didn't realise how loudly until the song had completely ended and Jeremy Vine set about carrying on with the callers.

"What is it, love?" John asked.

"Look, John." I said, still laughing. I showed him. "It was stuck to the bottom of my slipper!" John looked at me and smiled, then chuckled a bit the way he does. As I kept laughing, he just grinned, his eyes squinting at me, the white sky glowing through his thinning hair from beyond the window. My knee strained, so I lowered my foot back down to the lino. He moved back over to his tea and went to sip it.

"Oh, it's gone cold." He said, turning back to face me. I peeled the rasher off of my foot and threw it in the bin. I looked into the frying pan: the bacon was burnt, bubbling, the oil full of brown.

SILVIA ROSE

FIRST IMPRESSIONS

In the square

A red-head walks to the cafe. She wears black-and-white trousers and a fitted jacket. Her shoes sound out from the stone floor, each step like a wave telling people she's there.

She sits under the canopy. Empty tables surround her and she looks down at her hands, fiddles with her phone.

Staring at the cream stone statue in the square she wills herself to get lost in the history of such a thing. She wants to go exploring, seep into the outside world. But she flitters inside as if her heart is beating wings as she imagines Julia arriving, her soft voice vibrating in her ear, kissing her three times and saying sorry for being late. She imagines what Julia will talk about – Harry most likely, and what he's neglected this time – and wonders how she might respond. She can see Julia's long, brown fingers tapping her cigarette over the ashtray.

Checking her phone, she is met with a blank screen. She bites the nail of her middle finger too hard and it hangs, half torn, exposing a fleshy part of her.

*

Number 44 is a green-tiled building on the far side of the square. It looks like it was built in China, shipped over in parts, then reassembled. Its roof is thin and covered in yellow moss, with a narrow wooden door reaching all the way to the top.

A family lived here once who came from a country no one had heard of. They spoke to no one, but kept the front door open all day so that if you passed, you could hear music coming from inside. The music was quick and spindly like a spider spinning its web, with lots of strings and jumps in melody. The youngest boys would poke their heads out and follow your steps with watery dark eyes. If the day was light and you felt it in you, you could go up to them and give them a sweet. Often you would miss your chance, as a hand would come and grab their necks, pulling them back into the dim-lit room.

It wasn't until the music stopped that anyone noticed they had left.

*

Brie – if that's her real name – leans her elbows on the table. The mint-green of her painted nails matches her earrings.

'I was thinking about you last night.'

As she speaks, she looks into the distance and frowns. Turning back to the man opposite her, she blinks in slow motion, her eyelids lingering closed for a moment. It is an attempt to emphasize her point, to let the last word linger too.

When she opens her eyes she opens them wide and imagines that her stare is penetrating him.

He shows no reaction, only nods.

To push her point further, she screws the pointed tip of her shoe into his shin, staring straight at him. He doesn't move.

They stay like this for minutes, her screwing the tip of her shoe, him defiant and still.

Eventually she gives up.

'Do you like my dress?' she asks, her voice curling. 'It's new. I bought it at the market.'

'Too small?' he says.

She turns away, resting her chin in her hand, and smiles. It is the kind of smile where the bottom lip slightly overlaps the top, the kind usually accompanied by a sigh through the nose. It is a kind that says, 'funny, isn't it?'

'Why didn't you come and play on Saturday?' she says.

'I was busy.'

'Too busy to play?'

He grabs her ankle hard. She raises her eyebrows in surprise. Once again, they remain frozen like this. After a few beating moments he says to her slowly, 'This is *not* a game, my sunshine. You understand?'

His voice rolls across the table straight into her lap. She looks down, suddenly shy. He lets go of her ankle, seizes her hand instead. He kisses her knuckles one by one, scratching her skin with his stubble.

*

An old man crosses the square, dressed like a teenager, a green 'M' stitched on to his baseball cap. Though Marni is well over sixty, he has the assured stride of someone much younger. He throws and catches a pair of keys, looking about for a familiar face, anyone to catch his eye. He is on the way to the garage owned by his friend Gustav. They have arranged to play cards and drink beer in the back room, but Marni has other plans. He wants to drive to the lake where they spent summers building campfires and strumming guitars. He knows Gustav will agree to anything as long as there's beer involved.

He watches two boys ride their bikes. They wear similar caps to him. One goes up on his back wheel and shouts at his friend to look. Marni curses them through missing teeth.

Marni could tell you stories that would make you blush and pull at your skirt hem. But he is off to find trouble with Gustav, so he turns and leaves you with a wink.

On the beach

Pandora feels like a honey-soaked apricot, all juicy from the heat. She could melt right now and she would taste like a burnt dessert. Her boyfriend sits beside her reading a newspaper. He eats a sandwich and chews it with his mouth open.

She likes that he is rough and messy. She likes watching him play football and cheering from the sidelines. She knows all his friends look at her and whisper to each other when they pass. She likes that even more.

Pandora knows the girls at school look at her funny when she wears her favourite denim hot-pants. Her mother says people like that are just jealous.

Pandora was six when her mother first painted her nails. There are times when her mother looks at her as if she were looking in a mirror.

Sometimes when she rides the tram, she can sense a man's stare on her back. It feels like the compressed heat from an open oven door. It gives her a forbidden rush. Occasionally she will feel the touch of a man on her thigh, a faint brush, and the tingle of it stays with her for minutes.

*

Children play with monkey nuts on the pier, their feet dangling off the sides. They bite each one open by cracking the shell, discarding the woody fibres on the concrete floor. Chewing the nuts into an oily pulp, they spit them at each other, aiming for the head, or even better, the eye.

This game does not necessarily end with swallowing the nut. It is not nourishment they are looking for, it is the prize within the shell. Once the prize is found, that is the end of it. The nut is used only as a vessel for saliva.

Some of the shells fall into the foamy edges of the sea, and by evening there is a family of them floating, bobbing like overturned boats.

*

A green headband pulls back Karina's hair with a strict force. She is reading a book on Michelangelo and is so exhausted that the words jump around the page. She makes notes with a black biro. She doesn't see anything wrong with that; books aren't sacred. It is dangerous to put such high esteem onto pieces of paper.

Things that perish do so unconsciously. When a book is thrown into the fire, it does not scream or try to resist. Even the human body does not resist in the way we think it does. Yes – it holds its hands up to threat, and turns its head away from destruction. But the body perishes in an unseen way, unaware.

As she reads, she pouts and un-pouts her lips, an unconscious motion. Her lips are moving with her heart, in a way that reminds her that they are still alive, that they are still with the body, yet are unaware of their own inevitable ceasing, of how one day they will part in an accidental surrender, an outlet for the last breath.

She is on the chapter about his upbringing. Thirteen-year old Michelangelo is being punished by his father because he does not understand his son's obsession with art.

Karina once met a man called Michelangelo but he was a plumber and bore none of the immortal quality of his namesake. He had long, curly hair and spoke with a nervous giggle at the end of each sentence. When she told him that Michelangelo was her favourite artist, he responded, 'You know, I too am an artist. It's only because people cannot see pipes and drains that I don't get credit for it.'

She smiled, touched by the innocence of his joke, saddened by the way it sounded rehearsed.

*

Life on one side of the lens is different to that on the other. It is a life behind glass; the panting of breath amplified in a small box. Outside the lens is colour, noise, commotion. Inside, on the first side, it is still and innocent. It is mere projection of light, the projection of light which has not yet reached its screen. It travels, innocently, then reaches the lens and is met with a clear image. All the eye wants is to be met.

Grayson has worn glasses since he was three. Sometimes he thinks about what it was like for those three years and is glad he can't remember. It was life without the lens. It was innocent projection that wasn't met, left stranded in a space without borders or outlines.

Grayson still has moments when he wakes up from a bad dream, and feels trapped again in that space. His dreams spread themselves so thick that he forgets to reach for his glasses on the bedside cabinet and all he hears is his breath, slowing and fainting.

*

The book is covered in wrapping paper (African print: red, yellow and green). Old Mister's hands shake slightly as he turns the pages, awaiting the next word, savouring them like he's sucking a boiled sweet. The paper is starting to crumble.

He reaches a paragraph on page forty-two and stops, reads it a second time. It seems familiar. It describes the heroine placing a flower in her hair, getting ready for a dance. The flower is red with yellow seeds.

He reads the first sentence again. 'She held the flower, and stuck a pin in its stem as if she were making a daisy chain.'

Why did it strike him? Where had he seen this before?

He remembers his sisters making daisy chains when it was summer and the grass was long. But that wasn't it.

The words were tugging at a deeper memory, one that had become lodged under the rubble of other, more painful memories.

He doesn't notice but his grip has tightened on the pages. The image of a red flower being fastened on to a pin... It was so clear to him. He couldn't imagine any of the women from his past doing something so exotic.

What it stirred in him was like love in a dream; a tremor from an earthquake, leaving no mark, but felt in the body.

He scratches his neck, the folds of his skin tremble slightly at the touch. His throat feels dry and scratchy like he's swallowed a hair. He makes himself cough, it only gets worse.

In his mind, the woman fastens the flower on to a thin scarf tied around her head and leans down to check herself in the mirror, lifting her eyebrows to get a better look. He watches in the background without her noticing.

SAMUEL ROWE

MATERIAL

In the dream
of dissatisfaction
there is a drought &
seagulls rising
from fields &

when some weatherman
speaks of cloudburst
we stand in windows
hands clamming
rubber raincoat clad &

in some art gallery
as Egon we empty
ourselves in fluid
motion toward the folio or

canvas sprung &
compact radical
now nude now immobile
burning fluorescent
under eyesight

watercolour
parched &
waiting for
the downpour.

IN THE DREAM OF DISSATISFACTION

This lake is still & stuck in
a sifting smoke frame
thin & bound by

cruciform pylons:
a Salford scene in
Golgotha vein & I want you

to break Salford's Skull
under burnt sky
force

your face through this steel
lake wrench the surface
into ululation to

climb crooked pylons to
dive & bore
through the still

steel lake
face ringing clear
ripples out

to the bone wood boats
stiff & yawning
at the fringe of the lake

to the silent pylons
stood far
their shadows stiff

under burnt morning's wake
steel rising rising
into the mute landscape.

EMILY SAELI

GALATEA

THE CARDBOARD BOX WAS FILLED WITH CRAP. Crap that was carried tenderly on the subway ride over. Crap that was shielded from the rain at the expense of a good hair day. Crap that was balanced carefully on Raven's hip as she approached the door she had planned to enter for months. That's not to say that what was inside wasn't important. We can't judge whether Raven was silly for protecting a box of old shit, or if she was foolish long ago in the separate acts of slowly gathering the stuff inside. One cardboard box will not change whether or not love, and its accompanying symbols, are important; not to humanity, and not to vulnerable girls like Raven. It just happens to be, objectively, a box of crap.

Miranda worked in this particular shop. She was just out of college, and although she enjoyed her job, her degree was in family counseling. On bad days, it didn't seem like a true application of her education. On good days, she thought she was creating the foundation of families, and that was close enough. On the best days, she thought she was witnessing true love. She had a steady boyfriend, Steve. He was handsome and loyal, and failed her only on those best days when he seemed regrettably human.

The shop was called Galatea, one of a recently successful chain of stores Raven had read about, famous for "uniquely tailored results". Of all the things she valued in the world, today she had only her cardboard box and an appointment at eleven.

Raven pushed open the door with her free hip, set down her box on the floor and pulled her hair into a soggy bun.

Miranda couldn't quite see what was in the box, but the sight wasn't unusual for the job. People came in with boxes all the time, all of them filled with precious, meaningless things. Sometimes it was small boxes, filled with tear stained love letters, and sometimes they didn't need a physical vessel to carry mementos in.

Galatea specialized in creating "true love." Their motto was, "We don't create the love between two people, we create the people and let love do the rest."

"I have an appointment. First name Raven."

"Hey there Raven. My name is Miranda. I'll be your counselor for the next few months. You're signed up for every Monday at eleven, correct?" Miranda was trained in making people feel comfortable in these first few minutes. They tended to be awkward minutes. Facts helped. People wanted what they wanted but beat around the bush anyway. At one point, she had been instructed to say, "I see you're here to create true love," but, in her opinion, those words did nothing but point out the obvious void.

For Raven's sake, because she is not that kind of girl, we will not beat around the bush: Galatea serviced the heartbroken. People came in, picked strengths and weaknesses, entered in algorithms, and waited the month it took for their newfound love to be grown and inserted into their life. Opinion columns have fought over the morality of creating something for such a sinister purpose as love, and whether or not these "Andis" (short for Android, although they are flesh and loving blood) deserved any sort of rights at all. Critics argued that it fed obsession. Supporters ask if there is any healthier way to obsess?

Unsurprisingly, in Raven's lifetime, humanity hadn't solved true love, but instead, sated the question with legislation. Andis weren't to exceed a certain portion of the population. They could not know what they are. No one may purchase more than one Andi in a lifetime. In the rare event that an Andi were to ever step into a shop like Galatea, procedures were in place to prevent them from reproducing.

That first Monday they didn't even get to the box. That was normal. Raven continued to bring it with her, never letting the cardboard corners get ratty or bent.

Mementos weren't part of the process, strictly, so Miranda had to just wait for Raven to bring it up herself. Eventually Miranda arranged to have their meetings over lunch. It was unorthodox, but something about Raven's certainty of what she wanted–

"into movies, like really into them. Willing to illegally download them, and share with me. Has to know his way around a computer, both hardware and software components. Long eyelashes. Dark hair. Dark eyes, probably brown. Tall enough that I'd have to tiptoe to kiss him, but not too tall. Must be into music, but the pretentious, indie kind. Has to be strongly opinionated, borderline snobby about his likes and dislikes.

However, he must be willing to share and teach me about those opinions. Nerdy, awkward, passionate, sentimental only when it's really important. Logical to a fault, except when he's wrong. Mischievous. Charismatic in crowds, but goofy alone. Doesn't realize the effect he has on people."

–fascinated her. The Mondays stretched out as Miranda and Raven planned creative ways to create these components in another human being. They laughed and joked over soups and salads and anecdotes and formulas. They were great days, the kind that made Miranda sad to go home to regrettably human Steve.

There were two things they never talked about: what was in the box, and the breaking point. There's always a point, the moment when customers decide that they've had enough of humans and are willing to take control of love. Raven never mentioned the point, nor any specific name that put her there. She spoke as if her appointments at Monday just happened, and the box just packed itself.

On the last day they were back at Galatea, putting all the pieces together. As they were finalizing details and entering them into the computer, Raven finally offered to show her what was inside. Up until that point, Miranda hadn't even been sure she'd ever open it.

Raven gingerly lifted the top. She pulled out a large, soft, green hoodie, and a tattered Batman comic book. Out came a stack of classic records: Jimi Hendrix and The Eagles with Pink Floyd on top. A bright green wristband that seemed like it was from a concert and some yellowing sheet music. A ring in the shape of a bunny. A red and grey striped t shirt. Two handwritten journals. The bottom of the box was lined with books, cheap paperback editions. They needed the least explanation, but then, books rarely do. You shouldn't have expected anything special. I already told you, the box was filled with crap.

"It's sad, I know. So… is it what you expected?" Miranda laughed to herself.

"Kind of. It's not sad; I see things like this all the time. I never understand why people keep them though. I'm usually more of a 'burn it all' kind of girl."

"I keep these things… to remind me that I did love them. It's easy to hate them, hate what they each did to me, and to be cynical about love in general. If I hated them, then I'd hate what I loved about them, and I didn't love those things arbitrarily. It's not like these were celebrities, abstractions, I formed obsessions with. These guys were interested enough, at least at one point, to pursue me. I don't know where it went wrong. Some told me I was too upfront, but one told me that I was a pushover. For some, it seems like only thing I did wrong was fall for them.

Then they were done, they all were. That's where true heartbreak is, you know. Somebody once told me, the opposite of love isn't hate, it's indifference. Every single one of these guys has reminded me of that in the most painful way. But that's why I'm here, I can't stop loving, right?"

Miranda didn't need to say anything. She gestured to the keyboard, complete with an absurdly large, heart shaped "Just Add Love" button attached.

"Last step. Time to make him love you. Press the big heart, and then Create." There were several algorithms for "type" already programmed, but the final one, the one that identified only Raven as the object of his affection, was still waiting to be activated.

But Raven just shook her head sadly. "He's done already."

"Raven, sweetheart, you can't expect them to love you unless you design them to." She swallowed hard. This was what she had wanted. The one, invisible piece in the box she couldn't have shown anyone.

"Let's be honest, then I wouldn't love him. Not like that. It's not that I like being hurt like that but... I can't *make* him love me. Who wants to be loved because it's dictated?" She pressed Create.

Miranda was quiet for a moment. She considered the unethical, briefly, and then approved the build.

Months later, Miranda was wondering what happened to Raven. She was working a different shift, this time accompanied by a coworker, when a tall, bearded man walked in. She recognized him because she had been thinking about bright, beautiful Raven with her cardboard box for a while now. She quietly pulled up the file on the computer behind the desk just to be sure.

He looked at her with wide eyes. Miranda rarely saw the finished product of one she had ordered, and Andis were so common to see on the street that you never examined them as anything other than human.

"I'd like to order a... correction."

"Do I know you from somewhere?" Miranda blurted out. That smile. An awkward, lopsided thing that was designed to comfort, not entice. Miranda instantly knew Raven's heartbreak.

"I think you do."

An alarm beeped on the computer in front of them. A chip somewhere in his body was set to go off if he ever came back into Galatea. Miranda's coworker looked at her with shock and whispered, "He's an Andi. My God, this has never happened to me before. Stall him. I'll go get the procedure manual from the back."

Miranda turned back to face the man. "What kind of correction were you looking for, sir? You know it's not in our policy anywhere to correct true love." She was uncharacteristically sarcastic. It was the truth, but not the whole truth. They didn't correct love because they couldn't. Andis were programmed and grown, like test tube babies. There was no changing them.

"I know what I am. I know what I'm risking by coming here. I want to love her, Raven, but I can't. She created this incredible empathy within me but no way to access it, not for her. She said she wouldn't love me any other way. How did she do that? Program me to make me ignore her the more she loves me? She told me who you are, and how you helped her. Make me love her." Miranda's breath caught in her throat. For the second time in her life she considered the same, unethical action and then—

—her coworker ran in from the back doorway with what looked like an animal tagging device in his hand. It was more gun than computer. He stuck it in the man's neck and violently pressed the trigger.

Miranda could almost hear Raven's scream echoing in the short shriek that left her throat.

RACHEL SAMMONS

SIMPLE PURPOSES

THEIR FIRST DATE WAS ON THE STREET. Robert asked Emma what she wanted and she suggested something simple. So, late on a Saturday night, they bought pizzas from a pizza shack and sat together on a bench to eat from paper plates. By the end of the date, their fingers were greasy and their conversation was backed by the sound of wind in the palm trees and the occasional passing car.

Emma babbled about the job offer from Mr Somers and how he had criticised her choice to study photography.

Robert stared at Emma with hockey-puck eyes. 'But why would you want to work for someone who doesn't respect you for what you do?'

Her cheeks flushed and she looked down at her feet, in those knock-off Dolce Vita sandals. This was a self-consciousness that she eventually adjusted to as she spent more and more time with Robert. He became a companion for everything. They visited bookstores, reading first chapters of novels, and only speaking to each other when they left to buy plasters from a CVS because Robert got a paper cut. Then they spent rainy afternoons at the cinema, watching movies in an empty theatre and whispering to each other the entire time.

Robert's voice was wiry and thin; it crawled over each word meticulously, as if addressing a child. Emma loved how ideas were simplified in his mouth. She described ordeals to him and his response broke apart the complexity like a strand of yarn separating between fingers. He wouldn't entertain the impossibility of understanding an issue. Nothing was not worth an opinion. He offered her a taste of his perspective like a child would: candidly and without complication, but never without bias. Emma didn't blame him because it was in his voice's design; he couldn't help it, and she found this terrifyingly refreshing.

On their second pizza date, when Emma leaned in close for a kiss, Robert inched away.

'I'm sorry, Emma. I don't want any physicality until marriage. I need to know it will be worth it.'

This upset her because it made her feel like an easy girl.

'I mean,' he said, 'once you've had your first taste, you can't go back. If we kiss and then separate for some reason, I will long for that level of intimacy from every girl I date.'

Just like that, Robert placed his future happiness on Emma's shoulders.

Robert was the kind of guy who held his hands out, palms upward, to express confusion or not knowing something. If he were playing a character in a movie, the critics would deem him a poor actor because he spoke like he was reciting lines, with no stumbling or trail-offs. Most people Emma knew were so similar to each other in taste and demeanour while Robert seemed a different brand of person altogether, one that she couldn't imagine meeting ever again. She felt like she would recognise him anywhere.

They spent the most unusual afternoons together. They discussed whether or not voluntary prostitution was moral over nachos at the shopping centre's food court. Robert changed her mind within a span of three sentences. He made her mourn for illegal immigrants as they picked out wine glasses for his stepmother's dinner party. While they did meaningless things, Robert made everything in Emma's life sound meaningless. She stopped stuffing her closet with new clothes. She couldn't bring herself to wear makeup anymore. Even checking Facebook over breakfast felt pointless. With Robert, breakfast meant talking; pushing scraps of eggy bread into the cheeks between sentences. Emma treasured these conversations. She couldn't imagine feeling so useful without Robert.

Sometimes, Emma would see Robert with his father on Venice Beach, shouting to the potheads and reggae-rappers about God's Word. Robert called it the 'good infection'. He talked about the importance of planting an idea so that it spreads and consumes a person entirely.

Emma thought little about this until a few months later when, one evening, she shuffled into her bedroom and saw nothing of importance around her. There were posters of celebrities that she no longer fantasised about meeting. There was a kit for bleaching facial hair, a bottle-opener keychain, and a bra that matched her knickers. Emma couldn't see how this bedroom differed from any other one. It was like she had nothing left of herself. Everything that used to define her had been trivialised by the world that Robert opened up to her.

Robert never worried about anything. He talked about Heaven like it was the next step after university. It was almost cocky how sure he was that he would get accepted.

'When I think about God's promise to me, I can't care about spending money to get drunk or hating a person who gossiped about me because it all feels so insignificant,' he would say.

The simplicity of his life was powered by a higher purpose. Emma had purposes but they were simple – like, to be attractive, to be good company, or to be moral – and only now did she see how they made her life stressful.

It was Robert's fault. Before meeting him, she had been blissfully unaware of her shallowness. Now, it was only a matter of time before she became like Robert, quietly hating her simple purposes. Emma couldn't let him ruin the things that made her life worth living. He had God, she didn't.

She decided to go back home.

It was the evening that the storm began. Emma would long remember the sound the ocean made as she rode a taxi out to Malibu. The waves clapped against her ears and she shivered in the air-conditioning.

Robert's family had left to visit relatives in Pasadena but Robert had an essay due soon so he stayed home. Their housekeeper, Aracely, was on her way out and she let Emma inside. Emma surprised Robert in the kitchen.

'What are you doing here?' he said as if she was the guy intruding on the girl while she was home alone.

Emma explained to him that she was flying back to London the next day. She even brought her boarding pass because she felt it would keep Robert from protesting.

Instead, he slid onto a kitchen stool and stared at the window from the corners of his eyes. Raindrops crawled down the windowpane like insects.

'You'll have to stay here for tonight. It's too stormy.'

Emma had already eaten dinner so, instead, they spent the evening drinking tea in the lounge and watching a documentary about killer whales. Robert only spoke when it hit midnight and said that they ought to go to bed. Emma waited until she was told where she would sleep. Robert directed her to the guestroom.

That night, she lay awake in bed. The storm had only begun. She realised that a possibility had opened up for her.

With sighing steps, she climbed the staircase to Robert's bedroom. She nudged the door open and the hinges whimpered. Robert stood in the darkness with his eyes on the blank wall. He looked to her, almost with dread, as she stepped inside. She could smell tears in his breath.

His voice trembled like a thread.

'Why do you have to leave?'

So she reeled forward and pressed her cheek against his.

Emma played that night over and over again in her head on the flight back to England. It felt like a dream. She began to prickle with pride. Robert had never touched her hand or kissed her neck or held her against his skin. But that night, he decided to and Emma knew it was her influence.

She gazed out the window and smiled. While he had spent all autumn infecting her, she had now infected him.

SOFTFACES

"**V**ERTIGO! ARE YOU FUCKING SERIOUS?" Gregory said, looking up at the nurse.

Gregory was not a happy gargoyle. Gargoyles are generally a cheerful bunch, content to sit on their rooftops, funnel rainwater and live peacefully alongside pigeons – on the understanding that "live peacefully alongside" could occasionally mean "killing and eating". Gregory, however, was the exception. All week he'd been sitting on his perch overlooking the hospital gardens, his stone wings stretched out to catch the late summer sun, and all week his brain had been spinning and tumbling inside his head. Finally, on Saturday, he toppled five storeys off the roof and into the rose beds.

"How the fuck can I have vertigo? I've lived my entire bloody life on high buildings!"

The nurse, a young dryad, frowned disapprovingly at him. "I'm not entirely sure that kind of language is necessary, Gregory. I'm just passing on what the doctor said."

"Of course it's fucking necessary! Ninety years I've been up there! Ninety bloody years of near solitude. And now you're telling me that I have to stay down here until my fucking head stops spinning?" He collapsed back against the pillows with a gravelly sigh. "I *hate* ground level."

The nurse rolled her eyes and went to help the vomiting werewolf in the next bed.

Gregory's bad temper continued with the arrival of a fresh-faced, lab-coated vampire who stuck a metal instrument into his curved stone ear and scraped it around.

"Well, I can't see anything obvious that could be causing an infection."

"That'll be due to the absence of anything to get fucking infected!" Gregory snarled, pulling the blanket up to his chin. He did not like human-shaped things. Strange two-legged creatures. How the hell did they manage? Gregory had four legs and a pair of wings and he still fell off his rooftop. Why were softfaces not constantly tripping over, unbalanced by how few legs they had? What kind of witchcraft kept them upright? Who did they think they were, poking their little metal things into him?

"Well, if it's not physical, there's always the possibility of it being mental."

The doctor was talking over Gregory's head to another doctor, a woman who wasn't wearing a lab coat. Gregory narrowed his eyes. She was probably one of those... psychologists. His friend Ernie the hobgoblin had told him about them. They were head doctors, wanting to talk about feelings and emotions and other such girly things. Gregory had told Ernie, in no uncertain terms, that he thought it was a load of old bollocks.

The woman nodded. "I'll see when we can fit him in for assessment–"

"I can still fucking hear you, you know!" Gregory snapped. He was quite a sight, his lion-like stone face screwed up and his little front claws tightly gripping the bedcovers. The doctors exchanged alarmed glances before hurrying to steady a centaur who was recovering from a knee replacement.

*

Gregory had to spend the night in the hospital. He hadn't broken anything when he'd fallen but the fleshy types wanted to keep him in for "observation". Gregory didn't understand this. Observation was his job – his purpose, his reason for being. Why did they think they'd do it any better? He sat, silently glowering at anyone who dared approach him. When he wasn't glaring, he was gazing longingly out of the window. Gregory missed the cool breeze of his rooftop, the sound of the trees sighing as they settled in for the night, the shine of moonlight on his stony skin. He'd only ever spent one night inside in all his years and that was a long, long time ago in the room where he'd been created.

Gargoyles are not born but rather made, carved out of stone in such a way as to bring it to life. The art was lost centuries ago but the gargoyles lived on. Few are left, given the tendency of humans to replace beautiful old things with featureless shiny ones. Wrecking balls, explosions and chisels have smashed the gargoyle population into near extinction. Gregory had spent most of his life on top of a church in Germany. On the rare occasions that he did sleep, he still dreamt of watching the bombs fall in yet another human war. Sheets of fire had razed his city to the ground. His roof had melted under him, slipped from beneath his claws and cascaded down, taking him with it. Gregory had lain in the ruins for weeks, watching the humans and the other bi-pedal creatures creeping around the wreckage. Not one of them had helped him, despite his broken wings and cracked legs. Some had taken the stones from around him, the melted lead from the roof, the beautiful iron ship that had creaked in the wind.

In the chaos that followed, he'd been found by a clay creature, a golem, who took him away to some woods and repaired him. They'd travelled to England together, to this hospital for otherworldly and magical creatures. Gregory had taken up a new post on the rooftop, far away from any human-shaped beings. The golem had brought Ernie, a long-term resident in the psychiatric ward, up on one of his infrequent repair trips and the gargoyle and the hobgoblin had struck up a friendship. Ernie had taught Gregory English and brought him cigarettes. He was the only creature Gregory had spoken to since his arrival. No other fleshy types ventured up here.

In this context, it is not surprising that Gregory had developed such an unhealthy dislike of human-like creatures. They were, to his mind, worse than the ghastliest of nightgaunts. And now he found himself surrounded by them. He burrowed further under his blanket. Charlatans and frauds, the lot of them. He wasn't sure what they were up to, but they were definitely up to something. And it would not be good. "Never trust a softface," he muttered to himself. "Can't trust their wet, spongy eyes."

*

The next morning, the psychologist came to see Gregory. Her irises were the colour of a midnight sky. She pulled a chair over to the foot of the bed and smiled a small smile. "I feel like we got off to a bad start yesterday, Gregory. I'm sorry. Can we start over? I'm Dr Faulkner."

Gregory frowned and shuffled around in his bed, his stone skin rasping against the sheets. He'd heard about apologies from Ernie, heard that they were offered with the expectation that they would be accepted. But how? An apology wasn't a real thing, wasn't something you could touch, wasn't something you could hold between your claws. He squirmed uncomfortably. What was it Ernie had told him the response was? "I accept," he said in his gruff, scratchy voice.

The psychologist's smile grew, "Excellent. The doctors are a little confused about what's wrong. It's obviously not physical – they've never come across a gargoyle with an inner ear infection before. They want me to see if it's psychological, as in a problem with your mind. Does that make sense?"

Gregory scowled, "No. There's nothing wrong with me. I feel fine. Great. Fan-fucking-tastic."

"So your head has stopped spinning?" Dr Faulkner pulled out a notebook.

The creases in Gregory's brow deepened, "Of course it fucking has. Because there's nothing fucking wrong with me!"

He nodded, "If that's the case, why don't we head up to the roof? Get you back on your feet."

Gregory's stone face cracked into a smile. "That's the best bloody idea I've heard all day!" He threw the blanket off and leapt out of bed. He swayed a little and his hospital gown flapped around his ankles. Dr Faulkner reached out to steady him and Gregory glowered at her. He lifted his head up high and walked unsteadily out of the ward.

They made their way up the small back staircase leading to the first floor. There was a window at the top, a long one that let in a flood of sunlight. Gregory stopped in front of it and closed his eyes. He liked the way the sun warmed his stone. When, however, he looked down at the ground, his legs started to tremble. Gregory ground his teeth together and continued to the second floor, determined not to give anything away. The higher he went, though, the more his legs shook. By the third floor, Gregory's head was spinning once more. His legs couldn't hold him up and they collapsed, pitching him forward onto the landing. Dr Faulkner moved towards him, and Gregory growled. He tried to stand up, but his legs were shaking far too much and he fell back down.

It was no use; there was no hiding it: Gregory the gargoyle had developed a fear of heights.

*

By the time Ernie the hobgoblin reached the third floor, Gregory's face was hidden by stone fingers. Ernie sat on the step next to him, the three joints in his legs creaking and groaning like an old tree in a strong wind. He held a long pipe that let off greenish smoke as he puffed silently, watching the trees in the garden.

Gregory spread his fingers and peeped out at his friend. Ernie nodded at him to say hello.

"Ernie." Gregory croaked. "I'm fucked."

"Why's that, mate?"

Gregory lifted his head up. Little crystals of salt fell from his eyes and dropped onto the floor with a soft crunch. His face was the very picture of misery.

Ernie frowned and took his pipe out of his mouth. "Seriously Greg, what's goin' on?"

"I think I'm afraid of..." Gregory's voice got smaller as he looked up at the psychologist who nodded. "...Heights."

Ernie blew out a stream of green smoke. "Shit."

Poor Gregory's head dropped back into his hands. "What the fuck am I going to do?" His voice was muffled by the stone of his wings which he had wrapped protectively around himself.

Ernie put his hand on his friend to steady him. "Trust Dr Faulkner,' he said. She knows what she's doin'."

The psychologist smiled at Ernie. "Thank you, Ernie. Do you want to go back to bed, Gregory? Or you can stay here with Ernie, if you'd prefer."

Gregory whispered something and Ernie had to lean close to hear what it was. He did not appear to like it. "Greg, don't be a prat. It's not her fault you're ill."

There was another mumble from Gregory.

"Two legs, four legs, six, eight, it's no softface's fault. It's no one's fault, mate. The mind is a complicated bit of kit, sometimes it just needs fine tunin'."

Gregory turned his head sideways with a scrape and glared at Ernie. "Whose fucking side are you on?"

Ernie threw his hands up. "Yours, Greg! You daft bugger. I'm just tryin' to help you get back up to your roof."

Gregory sighed and looked up at Dr Faulkner. "What head medicine do you suggest then?"

She thought for a moment. "Probably some CBT-style immersion therapy." She sat a few steps below Gregory and Ernie. Gregory's stone features wore an expression of utter bafflement, prompting further explanation. "Which means, we'll slowly reintroduce you to heights, help you become used to them again. We may not know why you suddenly developed this fear of them, but I can help you deal with it. How does that sound?"

Gregory looked at his legs. Even now, sitting down, they shook, grating against the step. He didn't have much choice. There was no way he could return to his rooftop like this. If his legs couldn't carry him, there was no way his wings would be able to. Ernie seemed to trust this softface and he'd never led Gregory wrong before. He looked sadly out at the clear blue sky. If Dr Faulkner could get him back out beneath it, with nothing but birds above him… She held her hand out to help him up. Gregory took it.

SEAN SCANLON

CORONER'S REPORT
NOTES BY MR. SLATE

THE UNEMBALMED BODY IS THAT OF MS. MARIE CIMBER, age 36, a well-developed, well-nourished, and beautiful Caucasian female weighing 118 pounds, and measuring 70 inches in length.

HEAD

Immediately apparent is the morbid neck trauma. In this case, the specimen's head is completely avulsed from the body, with separation occurring at the cervical vertebra. Lividity is noted in the abdomen and outermost extremities, however Ms. Cimber's face has maintained a healthy pigment. The flesh there remains vitally pink.

HEART

The heart weighs 370 grams. It is a patently heavy heart, however there is nothing amiss in its other aspects. The arteries are distributed in the normal fashion, and all else appears in exceptional order. Blood almost pumps through this system.

LUNGS

Both lungs weigh within normal ranges. Whilst examining a section for mucosa, I lean across the corpse, accidentally depressing its sternum. As I do this, Ms. Cimber seems to emit a last breath. A stale gasp leaves her truncated windpipe, almost tuneful as it hisses from the stump of her neck. Quality of preservation is further noted.

DIGESTIVE TRACT

As regards the digestive system, both intestines are markedly empty. Stomach content is nominal, comprising a brownish mucoid, anchovies, two fingers of rum, and a rainbow of small capsules. In total, thirty-two capsules are counted. The tranquilizer Librium and its derivatives are identified. These findings corroborate allegations of DUI.

GENITAL SYSTEM

The external genitalia are without abnormality. In fact, they are pristine. I encourage the presiding coroner to forgo a vaginal smear, but he is insistent. Ms. Cimber was an unattached maiden, holy, and renowned for her gentle decency. I expound this, but the presiding coroner remains insistent.

'You're kind of prudish for a coroner, Slate – ever hear that before?'

I tell him clearly and firmly that the procedure is not warranted. I am a botanist and this is a rare flower – were it any other flower, I would gladly dissect it, such is my job – but this flower is *rare*.

'We can get a wetback to do it Slate, I guarantee you that.'

I am loathe to administer the smear, and do so with a delicate touch. So delicate.

SUBJECT SUMMARY AND NOTES

Death occurred for Ms. Cimber on the morning of May 3rd, 1953. The overt disarray of the specimen suggests spinal dislocation as the most likely cause of departure: in this case, the decedent's head was sheared off completely at the shoulders. Reports observe that Ms. Cimber was in a 'crazed' and 'violent' condition when she drove her Buick Riviera Coupe from the viaduct bridge on 4th street. The vehicle plunged 40 feet into solid concrete, resulting in a 'total'. The wreckage was compressed to nearly half its original size, in much the same fashion an industrial press would compact a car. When the victim was pried out, paramedics noted that Ms. Cimber's corpse was in remarkable arrangement despite these the circumstances – saving the obvious *decapitatus*.

By my findings, I will posit that her behaviour was probably caused, or at least worsened, by an overdose of prescription barbiturates, which were erroneously consumed with alcohol.

Ms. Cimber is survived by her parents Arthur and Izzy – both first- generation immigrants. She leaves in her wake a substantial legacy of music (seven studio records), plus more than two-dozen film credits, and an estate netted at over two million dollars. Her artistic output gave immense pleasure to everyone it reached, including this humble coroner, and the breadth of her achievements cannot be overstated.

Certainly, whatever it was that impelled Ms. Cimber on her fatal course, driving her to the 4th street viaduct bridge, and then over it, will likely remain a mystery forever.

The only theory I can possibly speculate on – and I must stress, this is wholly speculation – is that Ms. Cimber had, in the weeks leading up to her death, become profoundly disillusioned. Perhaps she wanted leave from Hollywood's cut and thrust, or perhaps, leave from life altogether. She saw death as her only recourse, and suicide as the express route. I have observed this in her countenance, which seems to show a bitter absolution.

There is something perversely divine about her, something both sacred and obscene that draws my stare, something both worldly and otherworldly. In German, the word would be *himmlisch*.

I am reminded of the kittens I once fostered. When I was six, I cared for nine white kittens. I mourned for them all in turn, but it was Snowy, the smallest and most precious of the litter, who crawled into a coal chute and was smothered to death. When my father pulled her out, the little baby was raw with soot, but her eyes still burned.

Ms. Cimber has something of that self-same quality.

POST-AUTOPSY SUTURING

I replace the organs and suture the body's cavities, restoring Ms. Cimber to a state of liveliness. As always, but especially in today's case, my stitch-work is painstaking, requiring an artisan level of detail. But I am diligent and tender. I thread each suture with savoured slowness.

I decide that some music might hasten my work, and switch on the radio. A bad idea. I forget that the system is faulty, with a tinny sound that clips and stutters. It is intolerable. This has been the case ever since an attendant spilled methanol over the speaker, damaging one of its contacts. I am about to turn the radio off when Ms. Cimber's voice strikes up. It is her rendition of *'I Got it Bad'*. The song is being played as part of a retrospective programme. It is followed by an elegiac oration (given by the radio news), and some more choice songs from her repertoire. Over the next forty minutes, I finish sewing, Ms. Cimber guiding my stitch.

At 11:40am, the presiding coroner re-enters with some news.

Ms. Cimber's executor has pushed for a follow-up autopsy. He suspects that his client's 'behaviours' might have been induced by an antidepressant called 'Pyrizan', and is requesting a sequential run of tests. This will undo all of my stitching. It will also necessitate an examination of the brain. I don't want any of that, but I especially don't want them to touch her head. It still holds that vital pinkness.

'The trustees are emphatic that we move her to Palo Oaks for a second opinion. We need to have her in an ice truck ASAP. The drivers will take it from there…'

I tell him that this course of action is ill-advised, and will compromise the freshness of the specimen. It would. The pathologists at Palo Oaks are butchers, and their freezer-engine is temperamental.

'There's no discussion. We've got twenty minutes to shift her.'

I restate my contentions. I tell the presiding coroner that Ms. Cimber is an angel, and that mutilating her any further would be a profanity – an affront to God.

'Maybe it's your brain we should be examining, Slate. Twenty minutes.'

He is stubborn as always. I try once more to express my feelings in simple terms. I am still holding the suture scissors. Heavy iron.

'Slate?'

I lift the scissors and arc them downwards with a fixed motion. They enter via the presiding coroner's nose, splitting it evenly through the middle, and driving downwards into the jawbone. Profuse exsanguination should be noted. The injured, 150 pound male staggers onto his knees and I withdraw the scissors to a spurt of teeth. I repeat until the action becomes a rote effort.

ESCAPE

I sweep the presiding coroner into a corner and attend to Ms. Cimber. Her frame, however slight, is too substantial to transport inconspicuously.

After a minute of searching, I locate a tennis bag large enough to accommodate her head. She fills it – just.

I sling the duffel, adjust my shoulders, and prepare to make a swift exit. Then, crossing towards the door, I hear it again:

'Like a lonely weeping willow lost in the wood... I got it bad, and that ain't good...'

It's still tinny and clipped. I look to the faulty radio, but the buttons are turned down, and the tuning dial is dark. I double take. I triple take. I slowly unsling the bag from my shoulder, and slower still, I drag its zipper open...

Quality of preservation is further noted.

MARY SCOTT

CORINTHIANS

(In memory of David Kato Kisuule)

W hen Beth returned from the rally, the doll was lying on her floor.
Strange, Beth thought, and stared at it, hands on hips. When this
had no discernible effect on the doll, she scratched her nose and picked it up.

It was beautifully carved, she could appreciate that. Every finger was
individually defined, every single toe on the sandaled feet. Actually, she
realised, there was only one sandaled foot. That was, there were two feet,
but only one had a sandal on it – the other was bare, and Beth wondered
what sort of doll maker would forget something that basic.

Everything else seemed intact, though. The doll was male and wore
a shirt and trousers, whittled so carefully as to have actual *wrinkles* – as
though the doll had been animated moments ago, supple and fleshed,
interrupted during an evening stroll and cast down into a new form.

Beth sucked on a strand of her hair and touched the doll's face as
gently as she could. It was oddly warm. It must have been lying in a patch
of sunlight, between one of the black bars cast by the shadow of her
blinds. The Texan summer turned the air to soup, even with air-con.

As though reading braille, Beth ghosted her fingertips over the doll's
features. Full lips, a dash of stubble on the upper jaw; ears that protruded
slightly and big eyes, hard eyes, set deep below a high forehead. Beth
followed the slope upwards, traced the course of the grain over the doll's
temples, the bald pate, towards the crown.

Towards the crown was as far as she could reach, it turned out. One
moment she was smoothing her index finger over the rise of the domed
head, the next it dipped, unexpectedly, violently. A splinter bit her skin
and she shoved the wound into her mouth, fumbling with her other hand
to turn the doll, the better to see proof of what she'd felt.

The doll's head was caved in, as if it had been whacked by a heavy soup-ladle, over and over. The smooth rendering of its skull had all been crushed and ruined, melded into a messy crater of splintered wood.

It was the violence of it above anything else, Beth reasoned with herself – the sheer force that someone must have used to make that impact. It was that that was making her sick; the idea of someone attacking an object that had been so carefully, so lovingly made.

Somewhere downstairs, a door slammed, followed by the thump of footsteps ascending the stairs. Noah. He never remembered to take his shoes off in the house, and the stairway carpet was worn thin with his clomping. His room was next to hers, and the door of her room was open.

Swiftly, Beth crossed to her bed and slid the doll beneath her pillow. It wasn't that she was scared of Noah seeing it – they had no secrets in the church, they had no need of them, and why would it matter if he saw it? She just didn't feel like discussing it right now.

'Beth?'

There was Noah, coming full pelt through her doorway without waiting for a response. Beth turned to her brother. Even in this heat, Noah's hair stood on end like a peach-coloured electric shock, bouncing as he twitched from foot to foot. Noah lived life in an exclamation mark, as her sister Rachel liked to say; calming him down was generally the first step to conversing with him.

'Mom, uh, Mom says she's making coffee if you want it? But you gotta come downstairs first.'

'Sure, tell her I'm coming.'

A quickly jerked grin and Noah was off again, a heavy beat of feet on the stairs, then an echoing *thud* indicating that he'd jumped the last several. Beth twisted her hair back and tied it with a band. It was nearly hip-length now, and getting raggedy at the ends, fading to the colour of milky tea.

The doll's skin was the colour of coffee beans. Beth thought hard of real coffee, strong coffee, pungent and hot in the jug in the kitchen, and followed the thought straight down the stairs. She didn't allow herself to look back.

*

Monday evening, a day later, and they were doing their Bible studies. Beth's mom ran the sessions for all the church children from the basement of their house, six until seven on weekdays and four to five o'clock on weekends.

They'd redone the basement for this purpose a couple of years ago, carrying down sofas and chairs and arranging long tables in an L shape. It was here that the kids now sat, Bibles open before them. Across from Beth, Rachel was helping Moriah to spell out C-O-R-I-N-T-H-I-A-N-S.

It was a big room, and the far side had been adopted as an area for the church's teenagers to hang out in, away from younger siblings (Beth caught Noah's hand before he could flick an eraser at Jacob.) There was a mini-fridge and even a TV, which blared mildly as they worked.

Some signs decorated the walls, including one of the first that Beth had made herself: one of their big 'God Hates Fags' placards, bright and garish with the American flag as a background. She was proud of that one.

Concentration dwindling, Beth stretched her arms out behind her back, trying to ease the ache in her shoulders. The night before, she'd woken at around one o'clock to find the doll pressing into her neck, having forgotten about it a little too effectively. Putting it on her bedside table hadn't helped, nor had turning it around; when she closed her eyes, it was there, and she had to open them at once, heart bumping, convinced that it would have crawled its way back onto the bed, be perched on her chest, grinning at her. At around 5am, she'd given up and gone running. It had calmed her, but hadn't eased her tiredness, nor helped to shift the deep-seated exhaustion now taken root in her bones.

She yawned.

'Beth? Uh, Beth?'

Beth cracked open watery eyes, to find Noah kneeling on the next chair. 'You okay?'

'I, uh, I need help with 15:10? Like, I think I get it, but I might not.'

Her brother's fingers were skittering against the table, gnawed fingernails clacking against the wood. Beth scooted closer to him.

'Okay, honey. Tell me what you think first, then we'll see if you're right.'

'Right. Okay, uh, so this first bit, 'But by the grace of God I am what I am'? Like, I think that means that God made us, like, as us? 'Cause he created us in our mom's stomachs and, so, he knows everything about us, like *everything*. So everything that we are, is by God's grace, like, it has his permission. Except for, like, sin and stuff, but uh, everything else. I think?'

Noah had his eyes fixed on her, expectantly, and Beth had a weird, limbless moment of not knowing what the heck to say to him. This was stupid, though, so she yanked her hair from her mouth, and tried to recall what Grandaddy had said about Corinthians.

'You're kinda right, Noah. God did create us in his grace, but you gotta remember that God's love isn't all that namby-pamby stuff those loudmouth preachers like to squawk about. God's grace is only as long as we go by his rules, you get? If we don't, that's it, you lose it.'

Was that what Grandaddy said? Yeah, it was for sure. He was a great preacher, all the elders said that; the only one in the entire country with the guts to tell God's truth.

'O-kaay.' Noah's frown belied his vigorous nodding. 'I guess I get it. But, uh, I thought Grandaddy said that most people are just, like, born evil? So they're not born with grace, are they?'

Beth cast a glance at Rachel – she was so much better at this than her – but she was still busy with Moriah. She rubbed her eyes and wondered how to explain.

Luckily, she was saved from trying by Jacob jumping to his feet and yelling 'Godsmack!' in a tone of unadulterated excitement. He was pointing at the TV, which was switched to CNN.

Beth twisted round to see the screen, and caught a segment of the anchor's voice.

'...refusing to treat it as a hate-crime, despite calls from local gay rights activists to investigate further. Kate Devlin is in Cameroon, with the story.'

A photograph flashed onto the screen. It was a photograph of a man with full lips and a stubbly jaw, with protruding ears and big, hard eyes. Right in her ear, Noah whispered: 'Is that a fag?'

Beth couldn't answer. Static had crept into the edges of her vision and her ears felt hot and heavy, as though she were underwater. There seemed to be a bubble in her chest.

She waited until the report was done and the anchor had moved onto chemically engineered vegetables. Then she stood up, avoided Noah's clinging, evaded her mom's questions, exited the basement and entered the backyard.

There she vomited, neatly and profusely, into Aunt Maggie's gardenias.

*

They had the same picture on all the webpages that Beth browsed – CCN, BBC, World News. On every new result that she clicked on during her fevered Google search, the same face met her eyes, and the same story was relayed.

'Cameroonian gay rights activist 32-year-old Stéphane Lembembet was attacked at his home today by unknown assailants. He was beaten with a hammer over the head and died on his way to hospital. His death is already generating international scrutiny, with some media houses linking it to his support for gay rights in his home country.'

There was a knock on the door.

Beth locked her phone and ducked under the bedclothes. The knocking paused. Then the door opened with a soft *click,* as she'd known it would, because there was no privacy in this house, none at all, and she concentrated on making her breathing deep and even, imitating sleep.

'I'm sick,' she'd told Mom, before begging off dinner to go to bed, where she had screamed into the mattress until her throat was raw and her face wet, with snot and sweat and tears.

The doll was nestled under her left arm. Doll. Was that what it was? He? The face was the same as the photo. The clothes were the same. On the news, a lone sandal had been shown on the floor of the crime scene. And his head—

Beth swallowed down fresh vomit and prayed that whoever the knocker was – Rachel, most likely – would leave. Instead, the bed dipped under a new weight and a head thumped down next to hers.

'Beth?'

Noah. 'Yes?'

'Are you mad at me? About Corinthians?'

It took her a moment to place what he meant. When she did, she lifted the bedclothes from her head to look her brother in the eye. 'No, I'm not mad at you.'

'You mad at Corinthians, then?'

Beth pulled herself up enough that her arms were free, free to wrap around Noah and tangle him into a hug. The doll ended up pressed against one shoulder, Noah's head resting on the other in a bizarre façade of protectiveness.

Beth closed her eyes, and thought of Stéphane Lembembe's crooked teeth, in his smiling photograph. She thought of the words on the news, 'fundamentalism,' and 'religion,' and 'planting hate.' She thought of the words on the signs that they held at rallies, how 'WBC' was as good as a curse-word in her classmate's houses, and how she had heard, in a matter of minutes, that a stranger across the globe from her had been murdered in his own bed.

She thought, *By the grace of God?*

She said, 'Yeah, I'm mad at Corinthians.'

ERROL SEYMOUR

RAT MAN

THE STINK OF GRIME AND OIL AND SWEAT ROSE UP from the depths of
the station. It weaved its way through the crowd and settled on their
clothes, their hair, their skin. Emily sniffed her sleeve.

"Dad," she said, tugging on the coat of the tall man stood next to her.
"It smells." Her father clutched her shoulder.

"That's the smell of the trains, love. The engine oil." He looked around,
and checked his watch.

Emily wrinkled her nose. The trains at home didn't smell this bad.
There was a rumble from somewhere deep below her feet, as though
some hungry beast was waiting to swallow her up. She buried her face in
her father's coat. It smelt of perfume. Emily's stomach bubbled and she
crossed her arms.

"Dad, the smell makes me sick," she said, her words muffled by the
thick black felt. Her mother never used to wear perfume.

"You think this smell is bad?" Her dad chuckled, as he reached down
and scooped Emily up into his arms. "A long long time ago, this station
was a sewer."

"Is that why there's wee on the wall?" Emily said, and pointed across
the hall. A man was sat beside the stain. His legs were crossed and there
was a battered old brown hat on the floor next to him. The man had an
even bigger hat on his head that cast a shadow over his whole face. Emily
turned back around.

"Dad, that man has two hats," she said, as she played with the toggles
on the backpack. "One has money in it."

"Good for him," her father said. He slid two bright orange tickets –
one for him, one for Emily – into the machine, and carried her through.

Emily watched over his shoulder as the man with two hats gathered up his things. He delved into the hat and pulled out a shiny new pound coin. He held it up to his face with a long, bony hand and sniffed at it suspiciously. Emily blinked. The man had a terribly odd-looking hand. It had four long fingers. Emily squinted. The fingers looked almost... furry. The man with two hats suddenly turned his gaze toward her and she buried her head in her father's shoulder with a frightened squeak. It smelt of perfume there too. Yuck. They stepped onto the escalator, and the man with two hats disappeared back into the crowd behind them.

"Dad?" She wriggled around so she could talk to him properly. It was getting warmer and smellier the further they went into the station. "Dad, you smell like a lady. Like Lily." Emily poked the edge of his collar to demonstrate. He batted her hand away.

"Look at all these posters, Emily," he said. Emily looked. Smiling faces surrounded her from all angles – people in makeup, in funny outfits. Big red numbers covered some of the posters. There was a 5, and a 0, and one that Emily didn't recognise at all.

"How about we try and see a show one of these days?" He smiled, and squeezed her ankle. Emily frowned. "What about *The Lion King?* You've got that on video." He pointed to a big yellow poster. As Emily looked, the man with two hats shuffled back into her vision.

"'Scuse me," he muttered as he pushed through the crowd. Emily's father shuffled against the side of the escalator to let him pass, but Emily was still so close that she could reach out and touch the man's face. His face was furry, too.

"What about Billy Elliot? That's got dancing in it." Her father was still looking at the posters, but Emily was looking at the thing under the man's hat. Curiously, she stretched out her leg and lifted the brim of the hat with her shoe.

Under the hat was the most frightening face Emily had ever seen. It was whiskery and sharp, and as Emily watched, his mouth opened, revealing a pair of large yellow teeth. She gasped and closed her eyes, but not before she saw the man and his terrible face whip around and pull his hat down comically low, so that the shape of his ears poked out of the battered leather. They were not like her ears, not at all. Emily heard a strange hissing noise, and when she opened her eyes, the man was scurrying away down the escalator, scattering commuters left and right.

"What do you think, love? We could take Lily along," her dad said as they stepped off the escalator. "She likes going to the theatre."

Emily scowled. "I don't want to."

Her dad went quiet – the kind of quiet he became when people came asking after her mother, or when Auntie Jenny came over late at night and stayed up talking in her sad, cracked voice. Her dad was smiling, but he had his eyes shut tight. Like he didn't want to see her any more.

"You can bring Lily if you really want. But you have to sit next to her," Emily said, as she braided the toggles on the rucksack into a plait. Her mother always used to plait her hair for her, unlike her dad, who always left it sat on her head. This time the smile on her dad's face was real, and he chuckled.

"Why's that then?" He smiled, taking the braid and wiggling it around like a snake. Emily grabbed it out of his hand and set it back down. This was serious.

"She smells funny," she said, and leant on her hand the way she'd seen people do on television. "Her perfume makes me sick."

"She knows a lot about the Underground," Her father said, as though Lily's knowledge of grown-up stuff made up for her horrible smell. Emily wriggled and wrinkled her nose again. Lily's perfume seemed to fill the air. It made her head spin.

"I want to go down," she said. They'd come to a stop now, and the platform air was thick with smells – engine oil, her dad had called it. He lowered her to ground level and gripped her little hand tightly. Not like Emily could go anywhere – her shoes kept sticking to the floor.

"Look at that," he said, pointing to a tunnel at one end of the platform. "The train that comes out of there is the one we're getting on." Emily didn't care much about trains, but there was a cold breeze blowing in from the tunnel – she wanted to know more about that. Then she thought that maybe the monster with the rumbling roar might live in there, and she quickly looked back down. She turned her gaze past the warning signs and advertisements towards the rusty tracks. Something was wriggling around on the rails. Emily stared as the little animal stood on its hind legs and twitched his nose. It reminded Emily very much of the man with the hats. She tugged at her father's coat with her free hand.

"Dad, what's that?" She looked up. He had seen the animal too, and his mouth was twisted sideways, like he'd just changed a nappy or spent an afternoon on the phone to the insurance company.

"That," he said, "is a rat."

Emily waited, but he didn't say anything else. There was a roar and a deep rumbling in the concrete, and when Emily looked up there was a train in the platform. She wondered what had happened to the rat, and whether it knew to mind the gap. Commuters and tourists bustled and pushed to get through the train doors, and soon Emily was back in her dad's arms, lifted high up above the crowd.

This provided her with a clear view as the man with two hats weaved his way through the crowd. He stopped behind a pair of men in business suits, and twitched and wriggled his fingers impatiently. One of the businessmen turned around and knocked the man's hat to the ground, sending him scrambling to retrieve it. As he did so, the shadows of his face were fully illuminated at last. Emily gasped as she realised what she was seeing.

"Dad!" she shrieked, loudly so that he could hear her properly over the rumbling of the train, "That man is a rat!" A few people in the crowd turned around with smiles that matched the ones on the posters. Had they seen the rat man too?

"Emily, that's very rude," her dad said, but Emily could see the smile hiding at the corners of his lips. She looked around. Nobody else had noticed the rat man worm his way into the crowd and slip through the train doors, his hat pulled tightly over his face. Emily shrank back as he passed by and covered her eyes. Maybe Lily's perfume smell wasn't so bad after all.

"Come on sweetheart," she heard her father say, "Not far now." She felt the crowd dissipate around her as they sat down. Her father put her down on the seat and she finally opened her eyes. The rat man was sat opposite, staring right back at her. Emily squeaked and hid behind her father's sleeve.

"Here, have a juice," her dad said, delving into the backpack and producing a carton of apple juice. He pierced the lid and handed it over. Emily took it and stared carefully down at the floor. An empty crisp packet danced in the draught from the tunnel and skittered across the linoleum. As Emily watched, a long, clawed hand darted out and snatched it up into the shadows beneath the rat man's hat. Emily stared as he examined the inside of the crisp packet, shoved his hand in, and after some probing, brought it back out covered with a few crumbs of green-looking crisps. The rat man's tongue darted out and licked beneath his long yellow nails. Emily handed her juice back to her dad.

"Don't want it now," she muttered in answer to the look he gave her. With a sigh, he finished off the juice in one slurp. He was looking out of the window. He hadn't seen the rat man.

When Emily turned back around, the crisp packet was in front of her face. The rat man shook it, insistently. Emily leaned back into the seat, as far away from his claw as possible. Up close, she could see that underneath his long, curved nails was years of built-up dirt and grime. She supposed she'd never heard of a rat washing their hands before. She looked up at her dad. He still wasn't watching.

"No thank you," she squeaked politely. The rat man snatched the crisp packet back before she'd even finished her sentence. The train came to a stop with a hiss and a rumble from somewhere deep below. It occurred to Emily that anything could be down there in the gaps between the rails. Maybe the rat man had friends. She opened her mouth to ask, but the rat man was already standing up to leave.

"Bye, rat man," Emily whispered, and gave a little wave. Her father heard her and shot the same look he used when she said something rude about Lily. The rat man turned and dipped his battered hat to her. In the fuzzy shadows of his face, she spotted a set of crooked, yellowing teeth. He was smiling. Emily smiled back.

"Dad, what other things live in the Underground?" she asked, when the rat man had gone.

"You'll have to ask Lily," replied Emily's dad. "She knows all sorts about the Underground."

Emily thought about this as she watched the rat man scurry along the platform. He bumped into a Chinese tourist who had stopped to take photographs, and a fat, pink tail slipped out of the back of his coat. The Chinese tourist looked around, bewildered, as the train pulled out of the station.

Emily wondered how many other people had seen the rat man. She couldn't be the only one, surely. Perhaps Lily would be good for something after all.

PORTRAIT OF A NAKED PERSON

I was warm when she drew her famous night
on my body, laughing
like the rain on the old playbill,
a while is too small to contain her;

All the NUDES are naked;
the legs and arms of them hover
as the chiffon slip over nothingness
and, 'nothing is yours if I fall for you'.

All the NUDES are women;
doesn't time seem to dress them
she says smoke is her mother's grey hair
while looking prone in the mirror
and, 'a moment is yours if I fall for you'.

All the NUDES are men;
doesn't time seem to dress them
she says she knows my last hand
that it'll be grey as silver
and, 'my mother's watch is yours if I fall for you'.

Walking, she is proud of her trundling heart,
all through her Montmartre
she says, Memory is too small to contain her.

TO LEARN

your manner of cutting onions
your patience for adverts
whether you would be kind to my cousins
who are only small, but growing, and may
be regular-sized by now. can you

sew a button? do you ask for advice?
does your mother hear about your day?
might you mention to her the girl
who moved her bag from the bus seat
to neighbour you, barely breathing?

TOILE

I can't imagine you in my room
sweat winding down the window handle
lapped up into a puddle
crumbs itching between my toes
dislocation called reformation
in your opiate eyes
tender as a flu shot
nothing I can't handle.
I can't imagine you
under these sheets
that I refuse to wash
with an empire of books
congregated in the corner
formulating our static whispers
into poetry for tomorrow.
I can't feel your crazed hands
flaking, as they unearth my chest
call me morbid – I'll show you everything
my tongue, a dead, saline sail
can't tessellate the words for you
as I gnaw on cigarettes
lighting and re-lighting
the stray hairs on your face
left over from the howl.
I can't call knotted hips
the pinnacle of existence
and I can't imagine you in my room
at least when I'm sober
wasted: all I see are iv drips
threaded round optics

hooked up to voices
we're alive
we're alive
no
not in my room.

HARRIET WATSON

THE QUEEN OF THE UNSEELIE COURT

ONCE, IN A CLUB WHERE THE RHYTHMIC *thump thump thump* of the
bass crept into the place her soul should have resided, the Queen of
the Unseelie Court hunted for her next meal. The club's floor was sticky
underfoot and the Queen curled her lip as her heels caught in a broken
tile. Long ago, she had stalked her prey through the twisting paths of the
darkest forests, or the soaring towers of the most royal of castles, but that
time had faded from the world centuries before.

The Queen slipped in and out of the crowds, trailing her fingers along
the exposed flesh of the dancers. The Queen of the Unseelie Court had
been created from siren's song, nix's breath and kelpie's hair and those
she touched felt their hearts twinge, felt an all-consuming and gut-
wrenching *need* to be close to her, felt their souls shrivel as sorrow crept
inside them and attached itself to their bones. The Queen smiled; her eyes
remained as cold and hard as a December sky. A single person caught her
gaze: a girl, small and slender and with hair the colour of champagne. She
danced as though on autopilot, glancing continuously towards the bar
where a man – her fiancée – sat tapping at his phone. He didn't look up once.

Niamh Caraway felt a hand slip around her waist and a wisp of breath
at her ear. She turned, and found herself staring up at a creature whose
very body radiated passion and lust and cruelty. The Queen sipped from
her glass and, pressing her lips to Niamh's, trickled some of the cocktail
into the other girl's mouth. Niamh dragged in a breath and clung to the
Queen; her skin felt like fire and ice all at once, she smelled like poppies
and hibiscus and lilies, and Niamh forgot everything else.

The Queen leaned in to murmur into the girl's ear. 'Come home
with me.'

And Niamh took the Queen's hand and followed as she led her through the crowd and towards a waiting car. She saw nothing but the corkscrew curls that spiralled from the Queen's head, the flash of territorial possession in her eyes, and so as the car drew away from the kerb Niamh didn't even register Andrew, throwing himself towards them, shouting her name. Niamh didn't resist as the Queen caressed her. She returned her cool kisses with the kind of desperate passion she had always been capable of, and even the Queen herself, the thief of a million souls, felt a touch of surprise at the ardour with which Niamh touched her. Gently, the Queen pushed her away.

'There'll be time enough,' she said. 'All the time in all the worlds is ours.'

'I can stay with you?'

'Perhaps.'

The Queen forestalled further conversation by touching one finger to Niamh's lips. The girl fell silent at once, the question she had been about to ask fading from her mind. Her eyes locked onto the Queen's, and almost without thought she poked her tongue and licked the tip of her finger. The Queen drew in a breath and slid her other hand under Niamh's dress.

'Tell me,' she said. 'Does he ever do this?'

Niamh's hips bucked and she gasped, and she still kept her eyes on the Queen's. The Queen smiled and kissed her savagely, drawing blood from the girl's lips.

'We'll be home soon,' she said.

For an hour or more they drove. At last they passed between two stone pillars, ten feet tall, each topped with a creature that Niamh could not see. The car drove on, passing through a stretch of woodland whose trees seemed to press together to block out the light, and beyond them a lake upon whose waters the remnants of the moon danced, illuminating the fingers of ice reaching for the unseen centre of the mere.

The car pulled up outside a house that sprawled across the grounds and stretched up towards the sky. The driver opened the door and the Queen stepped out, pulling Niamh behind her. The door swung inwards as they approached and a butler stared impassively at them.

'Welcome home, milady,' he said. 'May I escort you downstairs?'

A moment later, a second car drew up and Andrew threw open the door and forced his way out. The gravel seemed to shift under his feet as though it didn't want to carry him. He barely managed to stay upright, his arms flailing and his head thrown back in sudden fear. As he regained his balance, he saw the taxi leaving out of the corner of his eye.

He was alone.

The front door opened and the butler emerged.

'Please come in,' he said, his voice flat. 'The mistress is expecting you. If you would follow me, sir.'

Andrew followed the butler across the foyer and through a series of doors hidden in the elaborate panelling of the walls. The butler said nothing more to him until he pushed open a final door and bowed slightly.

'The mistress is through here, sir.'

Andrew crossed the threshold into a room ablaze with light. Fires raged in stone alcoves set into the walls every few feet, and Andrew caught the almost imperceptible hint of brimstone. Around him, clustered in groups of seven or eight, men and women stared silently, wearing masks made from lace and silver filigree and cloaks made of some heavy fabric that hung straight to the floor, fastened with a silver chain.

Raised up on a dais in the centre of the floor, a woman sat upright on a chair carved all over with intricate patterns. Alone among everybody else in the room, she was naked. Her skin gleamed, red copper in the firelight, every inch of her body illuminated; her glorious mane of dark hair tumbled down her body to full, firm breasts, each nipple pierced through with a silver ring; her lips, painted with a colour that defined everything that blood was and had ever been, parted in a luxurious moan. One hand caressed her own breast, the other was buried in the hair of the girl between her legs.

'Niamh!' The agony in Andrew's voice would have melted a demon's heart, but the Queen had only ever possessed the hearts of others and the cavity in her chest had lain empty since her creation.

She didn't hear him. She didn't flinch. On her knees before the Queen of the Unseelie Court, the Queen of Hearts herself, Niamh thought of nothing but giving pleasure to the creature who had stolen her so very thoroughly, her whole being focussed on the task.

Without ever letting her eyes leave Andrew's, the Queen pulled the girl up from her knees. Niamh's lips were dripping with blood; the Queen met them hungrily with her own, and only when she had settled Niamh back between her legs did she raise an eyebrow at Andrew.

'Can I offer you something?' Centuries of contemptuous cruelty echoed in her voice.

'She's... mine.'

'No,' the Queen said. 'She's her own. And mine.'

'I want her back.'

The butler, who had so far remained silent, suddenly stepped forward. He bowed to the Queen and climbed the dais, then bent to whisper in her ear. The Queen's expression darkened. She nodded at her servant and stood, sending Niamh tumbling to the dais floor, her eyes following the sway of the Queen's body with base lust.

'My butler reminds me of the laws,' the Queen announced. 'You have one chance. One task, as in the old days. Pass it and I shall return her heart.'

'I–.' Andrew hesitated. 'What is it?'

She raised her head. She longed for nothing more than to swat him as she would a fly, but even the Queen of Hearts is bound by the rules of the enchantments she invokes, and she could do nothing but nod to her butler. He opened another door. Andrew gagged at the stench of old blood that poured from the space beyond.

'In that room lie the hearts of my court,' the Queen said. 'Pick out the one that used to belong to the woman who used to be yours.'

Timidly Andrew stepped into the room. Rows upon rows of hearts lay there, beating still, thousands of them, because the Unseelie Court does not exist in one world alone and the Queen of that court of such a court has made slaves of humanity since time began. He bit his lip in sudden despair: all hearts look the same once out of the body and he could not even begin to distinguish which one had belonged to Niamh. He had thought he would have been able to see it at once, even if just because it was the newest, but some kind of magic had kept each heart perfectly preserved.

In a kind of daze, he closed his eyes and reached.

The Queen threw her head back and howled with triumph as he emerged. Exhilaration exploded within her and she was terrible in her victory. Suddenly she was transformed: no longer naked, her skirt was created from the hearts stolen from her court, her shoes were high and pointed and dripping blood, her hair was bound up in a crown carved from the skulls of lesser victims. Her fingers grew to talons; from her shoulders erupted great wings the colour of charcoal. She spat, she hissed; still beautiful, she became the Queen of Hearts in all her dark glory, the Eater of Souls, the grimmest of all fairy tales; she was the creature who had crept into the hearts of the powerful and razed pyramids, destroyed the Temple, scourged armies and never, *ever* lost to a mere human.

The heart that Andrew held crumbled into dust. He trembled as the Queen snatched Niamh into her embrace, enveloped her in her wings. Niamh submitted completely, and the Queen shouted at Andrew, 'Get out of here. Before I squash you.'

'No.' Niamh's voice was quiet, but it rang through the silent hall. 'I want him to stay.'

'What?' The Queen's eyes narrowed. She pulled away from Niamh.

'You want me to stay?' Andrew's voice cracked.

'She's right about you,' Niamh said steadily. 'She's given me more than you ever could in a thousand years. I want to become part of her court.'

'You can't!'

'She can.' The Queen sounded husky in her triumph. 'All it requires is a single sacrifice. A single heart, mine for the taking, in exchange for eternal life.'

Niamh met her gaze and the Queen understood what the girl had in mind. She turned and held a hand out and Andrew took it, allowing himself to be led forward with no comprehension of what was happening.

'You're sure?' the Queen asked Niamh. 'There can be no going back.'

Niamh nodded. Four members of the court moved forward as one, bringing with them coils of rope that they used to tie her fiancée's limbs together. The Queen of the Unseelie Court, the Queen of Hearts, changed once more. Her fingers grew, lengthening and sharpening until they resembled claws. She exchanged one final glance with Niamh and struck, slicing her fingers through Andrew's chest, splitting his skin, spilling his blood. He screamed, thrashing against his bonds, as she severed the veins and arteries that held his heart in place. She lifted it out, still throbbing, and held it high above her head for the court to see before turning to Niamh and offering the heart to her.

Andrew lived just long enough to see his fiancée bite into his heart, her face covered in his blood, her expression one of pure bliss.

ADAM WHITE

PLAYHOUSE

OR THE SUMMER SHE WAS BONNIE. Bonnie is an educated woman, not Ivy League like she had wanted, but at a nice liberal arts place in Maine. Modest, Bonnie will insist. Bonnie's father was a truck driver who ran out on her mother right after her birth, her mother succumbing to cancer a year after her graduation. Bonnie will call her father a bastard, though he will rarely come up in conversation. Bonnie's last relationship was with an older gentleman called Doug. Doug was broke, which confused Bonnie's friends. Diane is a secretary at a bank, and Libby is a stay-at-home mom to a three year-old, Jack. Jack is a biter. Diane has parties which Bonnie tries to attend; Libby is just so introverted these days. Bonnie doesn't understand. Bonnie likes to run errands and buy bread and does laundry and laughs at commercials for movies she'll never see because they're beneath her. She is twenty-nine and she is blonde.

Bonnie likes to keep to herself. But if someone were to ask, Bonnie would have a story or two.

*

The ad in the *Gazette* said they were a regular family in a one-storey suburban home on the east side of Pittsburgh with a guesthouse to fill. Bonnie answered the ad on a Tuesday and by Thursday had received an invitation to check the place out. On arrival, Bonnie determined the lawn hadn't been manicured, and she found the front door, coloured pink and crass, uninviting. But Bonnie rang the doorbell anyway; a noise answered by a slight, measured woman Bonnie liked to think was in her late forties or early fifties. She wore sunglasses and gardening gloves specked with debris, which she shook off once Bonnie offered her hand.

"I'm Bonnie; I'm here about the room."

Tess Dalton smiled and invited her inside, through the corridor and past the living and dining rooms, through the kitchen and into the backyard. It was unwieldy and difficult, tufts of lawn struggling out of the ground, buckets and broken toys like strays where the fun used to happen. Tess marched apologetically along the stepping stones to the guesthouse, embarrassed, Bonnie echoing her sorries with hummed compassion.

The guesthouse was humble, a door and a window, its messy blind fraying at the corners. Tess showed Bonnie the bed, which she assured her was new, its neighbouring desk with lamp and storage space, the adjacent bathroom. Everything was small, Bonnie thought. She smelled cleaning fluids, things with warning labels on them.

"You're moving here for work?"

"Yes, but it's temporary, potentially. I'm staying in a hotel for a few days but I'm interested in staying in an actual home, at least for the summer. Cheaper long-term. At least until I know where the job is going."

Bonnie told Tess that she was working at an accountancy firm downtown, helping out with company restructuring. The old manager was embezzling funds, and they needed to decide whether cuts are needed. Tess argued that it was terrible, the way big money constantly hurt the little people.

"Harry, my husband, he works at the steel mill. And they're just squeezing everybody out. Everything's going, it's just awful. But they must need you, if they're calling you in like that."

Bonnie smiled in recognition.

"The bathroom is small," Bonnie said. "But I'll manage."

Tess nodded enthusiastically, her face a mess of contradictions.

"We're really just looking for it to be filled. It's been empty for about a year. And Harry thought it'd be best we actually did something with it. I was quite happy to keep it how it was, but Harry's firm."

Tess wavered, her gaze locked onto the bed, watching the bare mattress and its bumps and grooves.

"If it's not perfect, please say."

"It works. I don't know how long I'll be here, so it works."

Tess guided Bonnie back through the yard and through the house, opening up the front door and stepping back out onto the porch.

"We're probably charging a little more than other properties in the area, I'm sure. And I wouldn't lie, or get you to pay more than it's worth."

"It's fine. I can get the money right away."

"Where are you from originally?" Tess asked.

"Virginia. Then Maine, but I've been living in Harrisburg for a couple of years."

"Really?" she replied, her eyes suddenly wide with enthusiasm. "My sister lives in Lancaster."

"I've never been. But I hear it's lovely."

*

It was on Wednesday evening that Bonnie received the phone call from Tess offering her the room. Bonnie noticed Tess's voice was husky, strained, as if she were sick. She made a note of it.

*

On Friday morning, when Tess and Harry were at work and Chelsea, their daughter, was at pre-school, their new houseguest journeyed inside of their home. Everything was in its place, she thought, and she matched the house's objects to its characters. A junk drawer of lives. Strands of hair on the bathroom carpet, lipstick for a wife, a sock in his drawer. Cracked glass from their fight. She had so wanted that doll, the birthday party. Yesterday's cereal, the milk that had spoiled, a diaphragm from when they tried. There were books, real men's novels, novels with titles like *Lethal Deliverance, Terminal Payback*. Area codes, prescription bottles. A thousand pains in a thousand different roles.

*

Bonnie lit a cigarette on the Saturday evening, leaning on the side of the guesthouse and letting the dirty smoke filter behind her. Across the yard and inside the kitchen was Tess, sat at the table with her hands splayed out onto it, her eyes bleary and raw, mouth wide and exposed. She was talking to someone Bonnie couldn't see from her angle, and if it weren't for the dark shadows gesturing like ghouls over Tess and the ceiling of the kitchen, she could have very well been speaking to herself. As she watched, Tess stopped mouthing things apart from the occasional grimace or depressed swallow. She soon tightened her hands into little fists, opened them up again, pulled them back beneath the table and wept. Bonnie stubbed out her cigarette onto the wall of the guesthouse and stopped looking.

*

"You're spying on me."

Bonnie felt eyes. The girl was a pudgy thing, Bonnie thought. All rolls and crumbs and kittens on her PJs. She stood in the open entrance of the guesthouse, tiny hands gripped to the door frame like she'd fall if she let go.

"Are you Chelsea?" Bonnie asked, putting down her magazine and reclining back into the desk's chair. The girl wavered slightly before nodding.

"What are you doing?" Chelsea asked.

"Reading and eating," she replied, nodding towards the messy bag of takeout spooling open in front of her. "You don't need to stand out there, you know."

"What are you reading?"

"A magazine. About famous people. I think it's your mother's."

Bonnie noticed Chelsea eyeing her food, and she offered some of it to her. Chelsea stepped slowly into the room, her eyes locked upon the stranger, before reaching out her hand and grabbing a paw of fries. She chewed neatly and stubbed a greasy finger onto the back of the magazine.

"I want that for my birthday."

"This one?" Bonnie studied the advertisement, "it's pretty."

The bicycle was pink and white, with glossy streamers on the handlebars. A blonde girl rode it across the page. Chelsea grabbed another awkward handful.

"But we don't have money."

"Oh, yeah? Well having money isn't so great."

"But you can get things."

"I guess you can. But it doesn't make it less boring."

Chelsea wiped her hands down her sides, streaks of stain and secrets.

"Do you have money?" she asked.

"Maybe."

"Lots of money?"

"Maybe. But it doesn't mean it's really yours. A lot of the time it's other people who worked for it, you just got lucky."

The two of them looked at the girl on the page.

"And it doesn't really mean anything either," Bonnie continued. "Buying things, that stuff, it all gets boring. So sometimes you have to find other things to do. And make your own fun."

Chelsea picked at the leftovers in her teeth with her tongue, and scanned the empty walls of the room. Bonnie followed her gaze, before Chelsea's eyes hit the floor.

"This is my brother's room."

"You have a brother?"

"Uh-huh." Chelsea peeked upwards again. "He died."

Bonnie's fries tasted like acid.

"How old was he?"

"Lots older. He was saving people a long way away. He made me laugh. And he'd put me on his back and it would be scary because he was gonna drop me but he didn't ever."

Chelsea stroked at her hair.

"I miss him."

Chelsea crawled up onto her brother's bed and turned to face Bonnie, her stocky legs tumbled over the side.

"Why are you in his room?"

*

Bonnie left the girl behind and made her way to the kitchen, stepping across the stones and into the light of the Dalton home. She only noticed the portly gentleman in the light blue tee and cotton shorts once she had opened the back door, the hazy light of the refrigerator's insides illuminating his gut, his skin fluorescent and charged. The man offered a meek hello.

"Are you Bonnie?"

Bonnie shut the door behind her, trapped.

"Guesthouse, yeah. Nice to finally meet you."

"I'm Harold," he told her. "Harry, actually. Harold's for people mad at me".

Harry expressed more a nasal exhale than a laugh, but his face still creased with tenderness. He stepped over to her, offering his hand. Bonnie nervously accepted, her other hand still tight behind her and attached to the knob.

"How are you settling in?"

"Fine, thank you."

"Good to hear. Would you like some coffee?"

"No, I was getting juice. I didn't realize anybody was up, I'm sorry."

"It's late. Tough to sleep."

Harry took out his milk at the counter, with Bonnie padding over to the fridge. She didn't know if her bare feet were sticky or if it was the floor. Either way it all felt hot and dirty.

"It's been a while since we made use of the room."

"Your wife was telling me."

"Right, right, right." The words seemed to hush their way out of his mouth. "It's a lovely room," he continued. "Small, but nice."

Bonnie poured orange juice into a glass.

"Tess keeps telling me I oughta stop drinking this," he said, tapping the top of the coffee jar with a teaspoon. "Bad for the ticker. For teeth. Brain too, supposedly."

"Don't they say that about everything?"

"They do. But I suppose you oughta look out for the warning signs. This stuff? It rots you from the inside out. She's right, though. She's usually right about those kinds of things."

Harry picked the kettle up from the stove and sat at the table, tipping the hot water into his cup until it was full, wrapping his chunky fingers around it and feeling warmth.

"It's good that you're here. I think it'll be good. For her, for Tess. I think it'll turn things around."

*

Chelsea was lying on her brother's bed when Bonnie returned to the guesthouse. She was curled into herself, so small that she could fit across the width of it without parts of her slipping off either edge. Bonnie watched the girl's gentle breathing, the rise and fall of her soft sides, the body nuzzled into the covers. Bonnie put down her glass and edged closer to the girl, her hands unsure but steady. She unfolded the blanket wrestled messily at the bottom of the bed and placed it delicately around the girl's body, squeezing it around her corners. Bonnie sat back on the desk chair, this chair no longer her own. She wondered if it ever really was, even for a moment. Picking up her glass and gulping a mouthful of orange, she sat and she thought and she watched. The girl was so small, so lost in amongst the blue.

Bonnie was gone by morning.

BIOGRAPHIES

Blythe Aimson is a second-year Literature and Creative Writing student. Originally from the Peak District, she is greatly inspired by nature and the landscape she grew up with but has also developed a fascination with confessional poetry since studying in Norwich. She aspires to publish both prose and poetry, and is working on producing a zine.

Lucas Aldrich might not be the 3rd in line to the throne of Monaco, the lovechild of Princess Grace and an Olympic rowing champion/sports journalist/professional alcohol enthusiast. He chose not to be involved in the Fall Hollister Campaign of 2012 in order to focus on his writing. He regrets this decision hourly.

Dara Arad is a 22-year-old palindrome. She writes nonfiction under the guise of fiction and poetry under the guise of prose. *Jungle Club* is a story about dreams lost and found in California at 120bpm.

Harriet Avery is a writer of prose, and a lover of words. She is about to graduate with a degree in English and Creative Writing, having thoroughly enjoyed every minute of it.

Isis Billing is a BA Scriptwriting and Performance student in her second year. She grew up in Thailand and India, moving back to Europe at the age of sixteen. Her travels remain a strong influence on her writing. An aspiring screenwriter, Isis adores the work of Wes Anderson and is a frequent contributor to *Concrete*'s film section.

Mary Blatchford is a 19-year-old English Literature and Creative Writing Undergraduate who aspires for a career in publishing. She grew up in Somerset and enjoys ballet and yoga.

Megan Bradbury wrote her first story, *Snakey and the Bright Angel* – the thrilling tale of a snake who is kidnapped by monsters and then rescued by an angel – when she was three years old. Whilst she fears she may never again be able to reach such heights of literary genius, she thought she might as well give it a go all the same; she is now in her second year studying English Literature with Creative Writing at UEA, and spends her free time reading detective novels, drinking copious amounts of hot squash (she's still in denial about being an adult) and planning her own episodes of Doctor Who.

Rhiannon Butlin is a 21-year-old final-year student. Born in London, she moved to Norwich to study English Literature and Creative Writing. She has written for her local newspaper and online; she named her blog 'thatpinksuit' after her love for fuchsia-coloured workwear. She is an aspiring copywriter and when she graduates she hopes to return to South London to attend the School of Communication Arts in Brixton.

Julian Canlas only started to write fiction consistently when he was 16 years old. Now armed with a trendy literary inferiority complex and perpetual fear of the ticking time, at 20 years old, his works have appeared in the Royal Collection Trust and several other small publications. He was recently placed third in the Geneva Literary poetry prize. He is currently a first-year undergraduate studying English with Creative Writing at UEA as a 50th Anniversary scholar.

Louis Cheslaw is a second-year student on the American Literature and Creative Writing course. He's currently slated to spend his third year in California, where he's hoping to find some new stimuli for his writing, as well as a great milkshake place.

Gaby Corry-Mead is a nineteen-year-old Londoner who has never managed to get the grime of the Big Smoke out of her eyes, though she can't say it's bothered her. She has been published in several anthologies and will have an independent e-book to her name by summer 2015. She hopes you enjoy her stories, they were written for you.

Jack de Quidt is sometimes a BAFTA-nominated writer and composer but is usually a confused heap of words piled up into the shape of a person.

Anastasia Dukakis is a second-year English Literature and Creative Writing student who enjoys writing short stories (shocking, I know).

Having lived in London, Singapore and now Norwich she is uncertain where she will end up next. If it happens to have a large bookstore, places to draw and a bit of sunshine she'll almost definitely be happy.

Robin Evans is a first-year student studying American Literature and Creative Writing. She loves the horror genre in books, films and games and her work is greatly influenced by John Ajvide Lindqvist. She is also passionate about impromptu adventures, animals of all kinds and mid-afternoon naps.

Milly Godfrey is a 19-year-old American Literature and Creative Writing student from Hampshire. She has been writing since the age of 15 and found recent inspiration in poetry workshops. After moving to America and then to Singapore before returning to the UK to attend UEA, her history with writing is sprawled across continents and often includes confused cultural references.

Anna Goldreich is an English Literature and Creative Writing student. Her favourite things are reading, writing, tree-climbing and avocados.

Rebecca Graham is in her first year of a degree of English Literature and Creative Writing at UEA. She was raised in West London but it was her visits to rural Canada that inspired the setting and many of the characters of her short story *Flies*.

Jennifer Hatherley grew up in London, but currently lives in Norwich. She is a third-year English Literature with Creative Writing student. She enjoys writing anything, but spends most of her time working on short stories and bad poetry. Tea is her creative fuel of choice. Her aspiration is one day to finish her novel, and she hopes that the endless tea consumption will help with this.

Joanna Hollins is a third-year undergraduate studying English Literature with Creative Writing. *All Day in Town* comes from her dissertation, a collection of poems on landscape and time. More of her poetry can be found at corybantically.wordpress.com

Ellie Howell was born in 1994 in Norfolk and studies English Literature. She divides her time between teaching, reading, writing poetry and learning piano.

Sarah A. Jones is one of many Sarah Joneses to study at UEA, and the older of the two Sarah Joneses currently studying there. She was born in San Diego, California, but was brought up in Leicester, England. She is currently completing the final year of her English Literature with Creative Writing BA and has been accepted onto the Writing the Modern World MA, starting September 2015. She is not at all concerned about her anonymity.

Nathaniel King is a student from UEA currently studying in Ontario, Canada where he is completing his degree and working on his first poetry collection. His work has previously appeared in *Lighthouse Literary Journal* and *The Elbow Room*. More writing can be found at askingthedust.tumblr.com

Lukas Kounoupis was born in Athens, Greece, on 24 March, 1995. He graduated from the German School of Athens in 2013 and is currently an undergraduate student at the UEA, where he studies English Literature with Creative Writing.

Francesca Kritikos is from Chicago, Illinois, the so-called murder capital of America. Somehow, she is still alive. Her work has appeared online in *The Fake Press*.

Miranda Langford would like to dedicate this story to the two most influential writers in her life. To JK Rowling: thank you for liking the poem I wrote when I was seven. And to MD: screw you, and your motorcycle.

Jo Lavender is a third-year undergraduate, studying literature and Creative Writing. She loves fantasy and historical fiction, both for reading and writing, and was inspired by Pat Barker's *Regeneration* to write about Siegfried Sassoon and his struggle with being diagnosed as shell-shocked while trying to protest against the war.

Katherine Leaver comes from the Midlands. She writes poetry and short fiction. Her suburban existence is defined by a futile search for meaning.

Emma Mackilligin is a poet about to complete her English and Creative Writing degree. She has only the vaguest of ideas as to what might happen next.

Victoria Maitland grew up in a sleepy village in the Norfolk countryside and, deciding she quite liked it, remained in Norfolk for her university experience. As a final-year student she spends her time alternating between excitement for the future and clammy-handed panic. She also runs a beauty/books/lifestyle blog (vickimaitland.blogspot.com). If you're looking for her in a crowd, she's the curly one who's probably wearing purple.

Greg Manterfield-Ivory is a graduate of American Literature with Creative Writing. He spent his third year studying at the University of North Carolina, Chapel Hill in the United States. Originally from Lincoln, Greg now lives and works in Norwich.

Amelia Marchington is a third-year Literature and History student. A very private pursuit, creative writing has caused Amelia to shred, and occasionally burn, many innocent pages. Sharing *Parasite* is a very surreal experience, one she does not expect to ever happen again in her lifetime.

Adam Maric-Cleaver was raised in Lewisham, London. He is currently 19. His interests include (in fact, are completely limited to): *Springwatch*, Cold War-era Chess Grandmasters and chips. He also enjoys playing with his band The Otherside. He is studying American Literature and Creative Writing, which, alphabetically speaking is one of the top courses at UEA.

Erin Michie is a third-year English Literature with Creative Writing student. In between reading and writing, her passions include baking, blogging and binge-watching *Come Dine With Me*. Her favourite literature of all time is J. D. Salinger's *A Perfect Day for Bananafish*, and recommends you read it straight away if you haven't already. She also hopes to one day publish a collection of short stories, if she can only learn to tame her rambling.

James Mortimer is a first-year undergraduate studying English Literature. His first love is scriptwriting, and is he's currently working on several projects, including a stage play, due to be performed in his hometown in 2016. His writing often encompasses social themes and takes unique (and occasionally surreal) perspectives on these. His obsessions include chocolate and TV show *Orphan Black*. *Bob* is his first published work.

Tatum O'Leary likes to write a lot, so she writes a lot. She is very interested in ideas of fame and heartbreak, which naturally makes her a huge Taylor Swift fan. She hopes her future will include writing and Taylor in equally generous measures.

Liam Offord is stumbling his way through an English Literature and Creative Writing degree, splitting his life between lectures on Shakespeare at university and lectures on cleaning his room at home. Home is Havant, in Hampshire. Writing is what he spends most of his time doing at the moment, and he's hoping that continues to be the case – because what would be a better way to spend a life than telling stories?

Lily Ozanne is a Mancunian who also has roots in the island of Guernsey and Vienna, Austria. She made her first foray into creative writing during primary school when she was selected to take part in a project funded by Excellence in the Cities. She attended Chorlton High School, where she volunteered in the library, won an award for a review she wrote as part of the Manchester Book Awards and had fun during several live comedy and drama performances (including one at Manchester Comedy Store). Elizabeth completed her A Levels at Xaverian Sixth Form College, whilst there she co-founded a book club. She was accepted to study English Literature at UEA and started in 2014, after a gap year of work and independent living in Manchester.

Molly Pearson grew up in St Albans, Hertfordshire, and currently lives in Norwich, where she spends her days writing prose, poetry and obscure combinations of the two. Her work is entirely personal, with no redeeming social importance. Sunflowers feature in it. So does substance abuse.

Laura Phillips is a final-year English and American Literature student. She was born and raised an Essex girl, is now rooted in Norwich but dreams of a life in Germany. She is currently writing a collection of short stories about her mother who passed away last year. You can tweet her @lau_phillips.

Jake Reynolds has been published in *Cuckoo Quarterly*, *Hark Magazine*, *Vademecum Magazine* and *Far Off Places*. In 2014, he was commissioned by Hands Across The Border to write a poem on the Scottish referendum on behalf of young poets in England. He enjoys living and laughing and not falling over.

Jessica Rhodes writes down things that are said to her, that she thinks about whilst thinking about things, that she overhears on the bus...There is a bit in the film *Buffalo 66*, in the middle of a bowling alley. The lights go down, *Moonchild* by King Crimson begins to play, and Christina Ricci does a tap dance. This is how best Jessica can describe the way she wants her poems to exist. After Ricci is finished, Vincent Gallo's character tells her to 'go sit down', and the film carries on.

Cailin Roles spent most of her young life in Florida indoors, hiding from the sun and reading. She now resides in Norwich, where there is no sun, but there are just as many books to read. In addition to her continuing series of retold fairy tales, Cailin is currently working on a self-illustrated graphic novel about her childhood.

Edward Rose is a fourth-year American Literature and Creative Writing Student from Essex.

Silvia Rose is a mixture of a rural upbringing in North Wales and Serbian roots. On the cusp of graduating from the English and Creative Writing course, she is both sad and excited to leave the cosy confines of Norwich. Her writing tends to be grounded in reality and always has a dark touch. She loves leopard print and beer and summer evenings.

Samuel Rowe is the editor of *Killer Whale Journal*, etc., etc. Writes poems about nudes, factories in Manchester, etc. Hates cooking.

Emily Saeli is an expected graduate of Hobart and William Smith class of 2016, with a double major in Writing and Rhetoric and International Relations. She visited UEA in the Fall of 2014 for one semester, but is originally from Orchard Park, New York. After school, she hopes to pursue writing wherever she can, but likely in a business setting.

Rachel Sammons hails from Chicago, USA and studies English Literature and Creative Writing. As a head-start for her writing career, she self-published a novel called *Toni* as well as its sequel, *Illusions for a Thief.* Lately, she finds herself writing about religious wrestling and what happens when the secular world collides with the Christian world. *Simple Purposes* is the short-story that made her first notice this pattern and she is excited to see where it goes.

Beth Saward is a third year student in English Literature and Creative Writing at UEA. Having just finished an undergraduate creative writing dissertation, set in a hospital for mythological creatures, Beth is still trapped in a world of urban fantasy, exploring the performativity of texts and the idea that how a text is physically constructed can impact upon our experience as readers.

William Everett Padelford was a prolific industrialist, inventor, and railroad executive, famous for his supernumerary fingers. Padelford served as congressman for North Carolina from 1889 to 1900. He succumbed to an infected carbuncle two days short of his 61st birthday in 1905. He is not **Sean Scanlon**.

Mary Scott is in her final year of an English Literature with Creative Writing degree. By the time you are reading this, she will most likely be crying out there in The Real World, preferably in the company of vodka. When not writing stories or making dour speculations about her future, Mary enjoys reading poetry, pining over the 1980's and befriending cats.

Errol Seymour is a third-year Creative Writing student and is about to go out and encounter this 'real world' thing everyone keeps warning her about. Her influences include Neil Gaiman, Sheridan le Fanu, and Haruki Murakami. When she isn't writing, she can be found staring deep into the void and roaming the lamplit streets of Norwich in search of cats to hug.

Leo Temple was born in Los Angeles but grew up in sunny Bridgwater, Somerset. He is primarily a poet but has been known to do other things.

Jo Thompson is a third-year who does many things, but is right now most interested in contemporary reimaginings of classical texts and ideas. The plan is to do an MA in medieval things at UEA and end up living on a narrowboat somewhere. The plan is subject to change.

Harriet Watson is about to complete her degree in English Literature & Creative Writing and wondering what she's going to do in the Real World. When not grappling with writers' block, she runs a showchoir at a local high school and sells the world's best gin to the good folks of Norwich.

I'm **Nina Ward**. I initially applied for the Creative Writing degree at UEA and was rejected.

Adam White is graduating soon and leaving all this writing stuff behind to get a proper job.